Scapegoats of society

The Underdog Matters

By

Ben Westwood

Contents

Introduction

Every now and then a person or a collective comes along and says "Hey, this shouldn't be happening to us" and at first they're often ignored. Initially upon hearing it people will tell them to get over it, but over time as each voice plays their part - eventually sometimes good and meaningful changes do actually happen.

Writing this book has certainly been an interesting process within a process, and has come about largely from my acknowledgement at the age of thirty-seven years-old of the stigmas that I've been experiencing for much of my life, but have only recently actually come to terms with.

Even when writing *'Poems From a Runaway'* which I self-published in 2017 I still hadn't even realised it, and despite people sometimes telling me of the sense of achievement that I should remind myself of, unfortunately there were many elements even in that journey alone that had shone a light on how some of us care leavers and those that have experienced homelessness can be perceived by the world around us - if being outspoken about certain topics hadn't caused enough people to shy away already.

Since first growing up into adulthood I'd always expressed to myself about how I felt a sense of solidarity and alliance with the black man and the gypsy. Yet if you were to ask me exactly why back then I honestly wouldn't have been able to tell you. But over a decade and a half on and despite having to come through the other side of many breakdowns to truly acknowledge it, I can finally accept that it's OK to state and admit that there's much unspoken stigma, abuse and exploitation of people from backgrounds like myself and say that it really does exist.

For all the positive and inspirational quotes that would be the type of thing that had actually helped me get through the process of turning my poems about my childhood memories into an actual book, I knew from the very start what I'd be up against, but not quite the true scale of it.

It had actually inspired me more than it had deflated me at the time, in which I embraced this sort of 'eye of the tiger' mentality with the Rocky theme tune playing in my head when times felt tough. 'Spirit of the underdogs' I told myself, 'spirit of the underdogs'.

The 'nothing's going to stop me attitude' had in fact eventually led to some interesting results after I'd sent press releases absolutely everywhere, causing me to collaborate with the Missing People charity through blogging as well as meeting other networks of social workers, fostering organisations and other care leavers. Largely though, the journey was a tough one, but that's life.

It's fair to say that this book goes deep at times whilst reflecting on some of my experiences, and despite not being able to represent or speak for all care leavers or those experiencing homelessness that all of them have their own unique and individual stories. Hopefully I can portray to anybody that reads this what life can be like through the eyes of somebody like myself.

Perhaps getting too heavy into the past on social media regarding some of the topics relating to abuse had caused a lot of sudden disconnection, whether through the algorithm or simply being too much for people to think about, and perhaps using the same platforms for everything was never the best way to try to promote my projects and concerns.

Still though, a small number of you have stuck with me and even helped support me whilst in the process of writing this book, not only through the odd sale or bit of support, but others also that helped in whatever way that they could to help counteract the feelings of a world that mysteriously constantly rejects and invalidates you.

Over the last decade or so I've been through a lot of personal changes and not all for the better too. Mental health can take its toll in the end, and in turn sometimes even physical appearance. Not that dreadlocks are the easiest thing to maintain but for some reason I constantly choose to avoid the easy route. But nevertheless, it can feel like a dark force is in grip and control of my life at times, a curse almost, as if life is laughing at me in the face. Once you learn to adapt to survive in whatever way that you can after everything, not everybody will always understand it, especially if they don't really know your story.

With everything that I talk about in this book, as well as the things that have happened in my life that I don't mention, perhaps in this writing comes other messages too about the misinterpretation of what should be called Post Traumatic Stress Disorder, but is often simply labelled as mental illness.

It's something that all of us can unknowingly do having jumped too quickly to conclusions, and not having heard the depths of a story from a person, even if we think that we're advocating for them.

There's a lot more here though than simply demanding recognition, but in fact a much more important message which I think the world would be foolish to ignore. Yes, the disregard, the exploitation, the stigma and all of the rest is very real indeed.

But more importantly if people really wanted a better future for the world that has less abuse and more connection, then perhaps it's important to see where we've gone wrong as a society in our lack of acknowledgement of the misunderstandings and the disregard of the experiences of people like myself. Ironically, it's not like there's a denial of such problems, we just seem to still go on to contribute in making decisions that allow these things to continue playing out.

Despite naturally batting it off constantly, it can still niggle away at a person eventually to know that often their stories, feelings and even warnings to the world are so often completely disregarded by people around them. It was a confusing place to be in for a while, but thankfully times are catching up with it all and I can finally feel strong in knowing that I'm not the only one that's going through this sort of experience, and that it's finally being recognised in society.

Whilst some of us contemplate if society really is breaking down, it seems that all of the things that used to mostly affect the unheard and unacknowledged eventually seep further into the fabric of everyday society. For most part, those that ever did go about trying to highlight the scope of exploitation, disregard, abuse, corruption and cover ups were only ever trying to do so as a natural response to try to protect others from facing the same fates as they did.

There are still a lot of people that don't see it like that though, and those that use the topic of abuse to follow internet trends and just join in on the hype-train do little to help the situation in that regard for survivors, whistle-blowers and abuse campaigners.

In this book I'll discuss some of the overlooked elements that are often part of such abuses in our society but rarely spoken about in current media. To put it in simple terms for now, we've learned about narcissism and psychopathy as well as the true scope of various forms of exploitation and abuse, but perhaps it's time to take a deeper look into both, and how they can interlink to create a reality that those around can become psychologically established in, thus causing them to indirectly condone such abuses and become bystanders.

I'd like to give a huge thank you to Kai the hitchhiker for giving me the opportunity to not only tell some of his story more authentically than I'd ever imagined I would do, as well as using it to reflect on parts of my own life - but also for correcting me on some of my own assumptions from being easily led to believe much of what I'd seen in the Netflix documentary about him.

I'd also like to thank those that stuck by me though my journey, of which it's been gut-wrenchingly obvious to some the mammoth task that it's been in getting my messages out there. Over time though, I've discovered some great people that I'm extremely grateful to have met since writing my first book.

Not only do I hope that this book is able to give more of a voice to some of those that grew up like myself, but for whoever else out there comes across the same stigmas and prejudices in society. For all my occasional bitterness that other groups seem to have been acknowledged for their stigmas more than care leavers and the homeless, a lot has changed recently in the realms of recognising them. During the process of writing this book it's been great to see those stigmas towards care leavers being officially acknowledged by some councils in the UK by introducing protective characteristics for them who acknowledge that many of us battle on in life largely almost alone.

In some ways I guess I'm trying to peel back a few layers of the things that some of us may already know but might not have reflected on with such situations under a microscope. Words, information and education are indeed very important, but how much of what we learn really provides us the fine detail enough for people to be able to feel and spot on instinct the workings of systemic exploitation and abuse at play.

Many of us would like to believe that we'd be the first to make a stand upon such dynamics occurring, but all too often people are screaming out that groups are turning against them, even colluding to quash their voice, and that any attempt of trying to do as what they'd perceived as the right thing had only been met with instant disregard, and with what can be interpreted as spinning and spiralling eyes in a complete trance.

I'd be lying if I said that when I'd started writing this book that I was in a bright place. But with the writing of it being an entire process in itself perhaps it's important to note for anyone else out there going through such an experience to remember that it's not all bad, and that most people aren't abusers or exploiters, just that sadly in today's world many seem to simply get spellbound by the Machiavellian charm which is often using many tricks. Just one of them in their arsenal is being perceived as the path to resource. I'll explain more about that later on, but the more I think about it the more significance I feel that it has in the world.

Sometimes the power is with those that are perceived by others as a provider of opportunity or resource, there's a lot at stake. Those that are more inclined to be exploitative or predatory will fight to the death for that position, because whilst respected and needed they feel like they can get away with whatever they want because few will cut down a tree that bears the only fruit around, even if that tree is rotting.

If this book goes on to help even one or two people become less judged and feel more understood, then it's been a good investment of my time to write it.

For those that have never knowingly dipped their feet into the oceans of systemic abuse, exploitation, stigma and anything else relating to it all - it's important to remember what those words actually mean. Perhaps on first presumption some would initially think that the battle is combatting only cruel slurs or dangerous social situations, but hopefully this book serves a reminder to some that it's a whole lot more than that, and it can affect almost every area of a person's life - from immediate relationships, employment and opportunities, and eventually for some - detrimental long-term negative mental health effects.

Of course, I don't have all of the answers or insights to every homeless person's life, but I hope to advocate for those like myself that feel they're constantly battling with an existence of feeling misunderstood by the world around them. Such experiences can result in feeling more exploited than truly welcomed in by the world in regards to it's true depths and when things seem to really matter, in which a somewhat vague relationship with the world can ensue despite a strong love and a natural wanting to care for it.

Upon hearing the words such as exploitation and abuse some might presume that those like me fail to stand our ground or simply don't pipe up enough to be listened to, which is ironic considering that most of us had survived and battled through much controversy during our lives.

With the current status quo, those like me standing their ground in such situations are rarely getting far in seeing any sort of desirable results or justice in their experiences. Abuse and exploitation is covered up far too often by the fobbing off that someone is merely paranoid or by labelling them as erratic, or as outright trouble-makers.

Even dealing with aggressive drunk people on the street can seem effortless compared to what gets flung about in what is apparently the normal world, which is currently infested with the destructive disease of control and manipulation over others, as well as much needless competition and battles that can feel like a complex game of chess.

Some people think it's normal, but I feel many like myself deep down had always found a way to navigate away from such realms that sacrifice genuine connection and collective health over the immediate sensations that a person can feel when group bonding has been achieved by 'black magic' style strategies.

See, you don't need to be old, frail, disabled or severely mentally impaired to be vulnerable. You just need to be largely out on your own with nobody really knowing your struggles.

Far from a qualified expert on the subject of abuse, perhaps it's still true to claim that those like myself that have experienced homelessness from such a young age learned quickly about being an immediate target for predators. Just like victims of domestic violence, child grooming and sexual abuse - there have been many times when it was someone like us that had quickly learned to see through the veils of apparent respectability.

One of the things that brings much magic and great vibes from the world around me is sometimes when I'm out busking with my guitar. People seem to enjoy the music and may see me walking through a town center that I've busked in seeming as if I knew everyone there. A nice existence on some levels, but none of those relationships are as deep as life-long bonds and it doesn't do much to counteract the feeling of being often completely misunderstood for who I am deep down, as well as feeling judged, disregarded and tossed aside as the scapegoat in many places that I've found myself in.

We're told that anybody can be successful if only they wanted to work hard enough, but money doesn't buy everything, especially happiness, and in a world where much more genuine connection and understanding among each other is often needed - many find their different ways of coping with the confusion through what can manifest as a variety of mental health disorders.

Sometimes people want to hear more about the shocking facts of a scandal than the ways in which we can be aware of how to prevent them. I'm not here to simply unleash the drama from life into a book, but in some ways it's an attempt to strip back the many layers that have gathered over some of our realities and take a fresh look at it all from other angles to get a deeper perspective on what's gone wrong in the world for a few of us. Of course, one must also take responsibility for their own failings, shortcomings and errors, but I really feel deep down that many among us have to climb back a lot harder to prove ourselves and be accepted for who we really are.

Perhaps it's healthy to accept that this will be a hard road in getting people to want to acknowledge it, especially as there will always be those in society that seek to provide an excuse or subtle validation for discrimination, abuse and exploitation. It's easy in today's world to see why some people choose to make their income from frauds, forged-fairytales and woven illusions because many like me simply become tired of coming up against such baffling barriers when it comes to being given a fair chance.

Some like myself try and keep faith through it, but over time that confidence can easily get smashed away when people link 'former homeless guy' with 'incapable.' How I've not re-entered the world of criminal justice somehow myself at this point I simply don't know. For what anybody might think of me and my struggles, I personally feel that I've done quite well in not having to tread on anyone else's toes to get by whilst watching others experience the many opportunities and moments that I feel I've missed out on in life.

It might even surprise some people to know this, as especially having been a young teen that had often been creative in learning how to get by on the streets. I'm not sure what's made me stick through all of this writing stuff to be fair, maybe the actual love for it. But despite getting into a little debt from time to time knowing that I've least tried to give it all a go in my most authentic way is something I can feel proud about I guess.

Whenever I talk about anybody experiencing homelessness, including those living on the streets, I certainly don't want to misrepresent or over-generalise anybody.

But I'm sure many of those people might agree with me when I say that what I had consciously picked up on from a young age whilst out there, was that it had often appeared that the most vulnerable of people, especially the elderly and those with chronic trauma or mental health issues that didn't put themselves out on show and employ hustling strategies could go much longer periods of time without people even seeming to notice them.

Being young back then I was lot more approachable, but once people get to a certain age all of that seems to go out of the window, especially when you look stressed.

Hopefully this book doesn't just speak for those like myself from a background in care and homelessness, but also for the many others out there that might feel underestimated, undervalued and in many ways unseen.

Any personal reflection of exploitation, abuse and injustices that I write about here are nothing that I need any personal sympathy for. However, there are many like myself that are sharing their experiences and shouting it out loud because we know that it takes people to listen, think about, care and respond for anything to change for those currently going through such events.

For many natural activists it's easy in the early days to presume that others will follow your lead, but the older you get the more you realise what such an established and mammoth task that you're taking on. Still though, you're often reminded, albeit sometimes years later, that what you'd presumed was a lonely and isolating experience was actually in the process of being played out on a much bigger level, such as when you start noticing in the mainstream media that voices are finally starting to talk about it all.

So, for all those like me that have gone through those processes of losing and finding their faith in humanity, and for a while were easily deceived into thinking they were alone, hang tight – it's a long game.

Despite the goodness there is in a lot of people, there's still a big problem of the homeless population being degraded in many different ways, with no real thought or respect as to how resilient and hypersensitive many of them actually are. Sure, they might not have the house, the long-standing careers and the mortgage, but what many of them do have is the willingness to keep going despite the fact that many have never really had any sense of support or guidance to exist and flourish in what is already a system hard enough for most people to navigate through and succeed in.

I guess I know that all too well by now. With finally acknowledging the levels of stigma and systemic abuse there really is towards many of those with a history of homelessness. Many would have chosen a completely different reality for themselves, but it is what it is and being adaptable humans we continue to survive.

Making a firm stand against a stigma that we know exists doesn't mean that we're trying to make a pity-party or play the victim when we question how society can treat some of it's vulnerable. Subconsciously though, many people still think that it's a world away, yet many aren't that far away from walking those roads themselves. Still, the disconnect between the two realities can give the illusion of more distance between people's lives than there actually is.

Eventually, certain dynamics reveal the well-established systemic abuse happening to sections of the community, and over time it can take its toll on some people, and its driving ethos's can even infiltrate well-meaning groups. It's understandably easy for those like myself to feel bitter about some of the things we feel that we've missed out on, whilst some can never understand what it's like to be largely out on your own, and how it causes you to be a beaming target for all sorts of exploitation and weird behavior.

Of course, it's a diverse world though and perhaps those that say you'll never defeat the predatory elements happening within our culture might be right to much a degree. But despite what some of you may think already, given a fair playing field we'd deal with those situations just fine.

But what a lot of people like me struggle to deal with and accept, is the world around us telling us that we're wrong for standing up for ourselves or others, which happens all the time, and quite frankly it's a baffling place to be in where goalposts are constantly moved and the game feels rigged.

Hopefully this book does its job of shedding more light on some of the situations that people like myself can find ourselves in, and the many barriers that we can find ourselves coming across.

Now even with **UK** councils recognising the stigma of the underdog, are you ready to accept this deep-rooted phenomenon?

Chapter One – My mission and aims for this book

"Stop trying to play the victim" some of them will say - "we all have problems."

For me personally though, I feel that too often it's nothing more than the echo of denial from those that are covering their ears whilst treating others as some sort of lesser species. I guess it's what makes some of us want to be a little nicer to the people around us, but many like myself are still trying to master being equally as forgiving to the people that have treated us like that along the way.

If those attitudes wouldn't go on to have such a huge impact on some people's lives, then those beliefs really wouldn't count for much from those whose concept of being estranged from their closest connections is somewhat of a complete alien one. Ironically, the 'put up and shut up' mentality which instantly disregards those experiences - caters only for those that it is convenient for.

Sometimes it's easier for society to accept what it's often being told to believe, which results in what people thinking they know being merely hearsay and imagination that is often a million miles away from the actual depths and realities of real people's experiences.

When systemic abuse is happening, it is so established and interwoven into a culture or a system that manipulation, exploitation, toxicity and mistreatment simply happens without question. People don't only condone it, but they even enforce it if such mistreatment of people is left unchallenged by the silent majority.

Whole groups will remain in complete denial that such phenomenon exists, and whilst the grab-what-you-can mentality has been left to run rampant throughout society over recent years, far more people nowadays are being exploited than ever before, and if you're losing the game then apparently it's all on you.

I'm all for taking responsibility for my own personal faults, but sometimes that's easier said than done in a culture that too often stays silent upon witnessing people being exploited or scapegoated. Perhaps it's time to take a much deeper view on homelessness before we can create that bigger bridge and connection needed in order to create a system that means people get a much better chance at living normal lives.

It's all good for people to talk about how they helped a homeless person once or that they can empathise because they had nowhere to stay for a few weeks at some point in their own lives, but this book is about getting into some of the real ins-and-outs of the common care leaver and homeless experience. The exploitation, corruption and failing homeless systems can completely shatter the confidence of a person if the mental health effects are left to grow for too long, because it creates a completely negative perception of people that have been through enough already, but constantly find themselves getting judged because of it.

Of course, like all groups and populations, not all among us are complete angels, especially considering the serious damage and trauma that some people have experienced from such a young age, with many stories that would make my own one look like a walk in the park.

Despite some of the more damaged among us learning how to survive by using manipulation tactics and deceit, for most part many still wear their hearts on their sleeves, unlike some of the shadier elements of the seemingly regular world where people can hide their disturbing issues often with a lot more ease by blending in with the status quo and using the illusion of group bonding, charm and respectability.

Learning of the stigma some of us within this society will face certainly takes more than just a few conversations. It can in fact take decades of someone constantly being discriminated against before they've even realised what's actually going on, which can come with much confusion and unguided quests for answers. Despite the obvious effects to employment and career progression, those that are largely out on their own and also find themselves without any sense of real purpose in their lives can and often do go on to develop a whole host of addictions and mental health effects.

It's a competitive world out there for sure, but much of it in today's climate can be completely needless and self-defeating. Some us are craving for more natural team players in key positions that want to rid environments of the exploitative and toxic elements that poison them.

Despite such toxicity perhaps not being in the majority of people - when left unchallenged it can cause enough damage to the depths of an environment that it might as well be. Too often in an era with ever-growing Machiavellian influences we rarely see through the masks and charm of those that will throw anyone under the bus to get ahead or even just for fun, and often it will be people from backgrounds like my own that find themselves forever fighting in a world where they simply just want to get on with their lives in peace.

Like many others, most of my experiences seeking help from the mental health system when I've needed it the most has been tragic to say the least.

I believe that one of our most major shortcomings within it has been the failure for many trained mental health workers to simply put themselves in the shoes of some of the people that have been going to them for the support that they need. That's often been my experience and that of some of the people that I know at least anyway.

Despite being a frequent runaway as a teen and living in care, my only actual experiences of any obvious interactions with mental health professions in my youth had been at the age of ten years old when I'd go with my mum to the family psychologists to try and solve the problem of me running away. But after a few visits spanning several months which had consisted of me sitting in a room with cameras and microphones with psychologists, as well as a technician and an analyst sat behind two-way mirrors, it seemed that in the end everyone involved had remained stuck for answers.

Perhaps if I'd have been born a few years later they might have given me some mental health disorder label or something, but then again perhaps I was just one of many of us that were symptoms of the world outside being a little ill, a mix of unfortunate situations so to speak.

Without asking for a big shiny badge, I'm quite certain that like many people from similar walks of life that I'm one of those with ADHD or some form of autism or whatnot, but these things can be difficult to pinpoint when the cognitive effects consist of some of the same identical ones as PTSD, but perhaps it might explain the many miles walked and weeks staying awake as a young runaway kid.

Despite feeling from experience that there can be a complete disregard for it though, I would have thought that many of the situations that I'd been through on the streets growing up would certainly create some forms of PTSD.

Those like myself which fall out of the system whilst battling disregarded and undiagnosed mental health difficulties will only likely go on to develop even more issues created from the stress and anxieties of simply ploughing on through it.

Whilst some people successfully create their support networks and forms of tribalism over their depression, anxiety, ADHD and autism labels, there are others from walks of life like my own that will rarely ever get a look in with such sorts of groups.

Even in the world of mental health advocacy we can be pushed to the back of the queue, still not seen as worthy enough of the being listening to and rarely ever taken seriously, even when going above and beyond to explain problems and proactive paths to solutions.

Fingers crossed though that one day this will change, but the fact that so many people like myself are often feeling completely invisible speaks volumes about the levels of disconnection that we're experiencing in society as a whole.

Whilst those society deems as worthy enough to get the support they need, those people are often much more likely to get taken seriously in certain circumstances. For others that might not have appeared to fit in with the norm, they'll be simply given anti-psychotics and diagnoses based on ten-minute conversations.

Sometimes people are seeking mental health support because of the things that they're going through at the time too though, and heaven forbid anybody like myself claims that they've been harassed, stitched-up, stalked or anything of the like - because for all of the headlines, articles and videos that try to help society gain a progressive understanding of those issues, whilst such circumstances can appear as shocking when it happens to other people, when it happens to us people just don't bat an eyelid.

It's all too easy to look at a person's circumstances and presume that it's all down to a complete lack of motivation, stupidity, or a drug addiction. I'm hoping that this book brings about just a little more respect for those that have gone through so many of their biggest struggles almost completely alone and with often nobody at all really knowing about them.

Although I know there is always someone that had it a lot worse than I did, and I'm hoping that the spiral of depression that those like myself can find ourselves in because of the current attitudes can become that little bit more understandable. Especially with so many having to navigate through serious depression and even cognitive damage from an early age.

Some people have even seemed surprised when I've explained to them that when at my worst levels of depression, my experiences can give me similar effects to feeling drunk, which in turn sends my normal cognitive focus into complete obliteration. Not being able to type on a computer keyboard and bumping into things a lot more easily are just a couple of the symptoms of it, and that's simply through depression alone! Some of you will know exactly what I'm on about, but there are still those which find it surprising that those affects exist in me.

Those quick to invalidate such experiences will no doubt try to pin this on the effects of substance abuse, but I can categorically say that it has nothing to do with it. Yet, such levels of depression can create the visible symptoms that appear as if somebody was under the influence of depressive drugs or alcohol.

As for exploitation, stalking, narcissism, psychopathy and the many other forms of predatory dynamics that can affect people's lives, again - my experience has been that regarding those like myself ever calling it out we're nearly always simply instantly invalidated, in which even our loudest calls consistently go over most people's heads, safeguarding professionals included. Time after time, after time, after time.

Still to this day it's often difficult for me to work out whether people are simply unaware when it's happening, or if they simply don't care. Too many events regarding exploitation and abuse are only ever heard about in headlines or on the TV, giving the illusion that it only happens to other people and never to us.

Some of those most dedicated police officers around will tell you a completely different story however, of which unfortunately people aren't always too interested in hearing because it hasn't been sensationalized enough. Any closer to home and perhaps a bit of post-digestion recovery time might be needed depending on the severity of things.

And yet here we are, one of the groups most at obvious risk of exploitation and for being a target of a whole variety of schemes which eventually become normalized. Many of us have been shouting it out on show for the world to hear, but still it all continues to get pushed back behind the curtains unless it's a vague enough statement to serve those that can benefit somehow for all of the wrong reasons.

"Nothing happening here, move along now please, the world has bigger problems. Nobody cares about them, so why should we?" is the reality and response that quite a few people can face, either through words or actions. The irony is unbelievable.

Racism happens, homophobia happens, but as for those often at the bottom of the social and economic ladder there seems so little reflection on their inclusion and equality within society, or of the needless barriers that they face based on the prejudice and discrimination they can experience.

As for others, including those at the other end of the financial spectrum that might be going out of their way to help the homeless in one form or another, it's great to see people spreading the love and coming together to support those that obviously need it. But regarding the bigger picture, something deeper needs to change regarding our solving of homelessness, and I believe that despite the funding being necessary to create and operate an efficient system to prevent it, it's also about how that money is spent and how it enables people to create meaningful lives and futures for themselves.

Regarding progression in attitudes towards care leavers and the homeless, could you imagine if nothing had ever changed back in the slave trade days and today's perceptions of acts of kindness was to simply give people an extra meal or a slightly more comfortable set of chains during transit? Yet because of a complete denial of our many failing systems and a frequent disregard of complex social problems, our one-size-fits-all approach to reducing homelessness might actually be creating more problems than it helps to solve.

If there were more mental health professionals and police officers however that were naturally drawn to being aware of what happens in the often unseen world's from the perspective of a person living through it, then perhaps the numerous scandals of police mistreatment that happen to people from certain demographics wouldn't be coming out every few years. Perhaps instead of being completely stunned and baffled at the reaction of others to such serious matters by being told that our events are taken out of context, irrelevant or that 'we must have got it wrong' would actually start getting listened to, because those are the typical sorts of reactions that we get.

Perhaps it's not until you've experienced the hellish reality of so few people taking what you say seriously, and on a frequent basis, that you can truly comprehend how large the scope of such needless failings is here in the UK, as well as other parts of the world.

Feeling disrespected, undervalued, misunderstood, not taken seriously and scapegoated are no doubt perhaps some of the frequent darker feelings that can be experienced by many of us.

Perhaps it's all too easy in this ever-busy world for people to expect the simple answers to what are often complex problems. Among those that haven't really experienced homelessness it's all too easy to presume that all a person has to do is go to the council and they'll magically get some sort of emergency help, otherwise known by people not so much on the grapevine as 'one of those hostel places or something.'

Even having a secure job often doesn't solve the immediate issue of homelessness for many people in today's world without the right steps in place to make accessing safe and affordable housing options swift and efficient for those without the typical set of references, and despite the resilience shown by those that can keep it all together, some may have better luck than others trying to find a way out of their situation.

But those among us that have knowingly or unknowingly experienced discrimination in many of its forms will know that the book certainly doesn't stop at people not understanding what it can be like to frequently come across those barriers.

I'm going to say what many of you already know deep down but few want to really believe – That people with irregular backgrounds, care leavers, those with mental health problems and histories of homelessness are forever getting stitched up and muscled out of jobs and projects.

In a world where a lot of people feel completely desperate to keep their jobs but rarely admit it, as well as the deep-rooted lust for controlling others in significant amounts of the population, too often people deny that such conspiracies to control the narrative in the workplace happen. But they do happen, all of the time and every day across the country if not the whole western world.

The gradual hammering away at the self-confidence of learning that you'll nearly always be among the first of people to be thrown under the bus can have detrimental effects. Often something much deeper is getting in the way of seeing things for what they truly are by those in key positions that are making the critical decisions that affect peoples lives in response to such workplace games and Machiavellianism.

A lot of care leavers are some of the most outgoing people that you'll ever meet, but at times can be seen as a threat, or dispensable, in a world where people's main priority can be getting a job position for a friend or progressing up the career ladder. Let's make no bones about it, it's a cut-throat world out there at times where often the most ruthless are getting ahead, and despite the baffling reaction by some of us that snakey and Machiavellian tricks work on people, unfortunately they actually do.

.

What a lot of people fail to see is an immediate and subconscious undervaluing whenever somebody like myself is trying to stand their ground against discriminations and ill behaviours that they face towards them in seemingly regular and established environments. It can too often result in being left in a position where we simply can't win whatever we say or do, whilst it can seem that everyone else around simply panders to the will of the game-players and narcissists, even though it would appear that everybody knows exactly what's being played out.

You'd hope that if you say your piece enough and show everything for what it is that things might get easier for you, but it's a lot easier said than done in environments that consist of domineering personalities and those with an over-bearing lust to control the workplace narratives around them.

The degrading tones that can surface from time to time from some of those with a two-dimensional perspective of trauma can be clear to those that have had their eyes opened to real prejudice in one way or another.

Unfortunately, some will never learn to understand it at all, in which spiteful and uneducated attitudes towards those from lives like my own can surface from seemingly respectable adults. For those unaware of it being played out it can be bliss to much of a degree, but stigma and discrimination doesn't always happen right in front of people's eyes, nor does everyone always show their true cards in a world where you so often have to be careful who to trust.

Despite such life experiences bringing their own sets of advantages, it can be a tough situation to deal with when you realise important life situations have been getting manipulated by silent assassins. It's something that many different people from all walks of life can experience and not just those with histories like my own, but being seen as vulnerable prey by the more narcissist personalities out there and forever finding ourselves in battles with them is really no easy feat. Even more so for those in extremely isolated circumstances, which many from backgrounds like mine are.

Unfortunately, I've come to learn that what I once thought would be some sort of respect that I'd get from sharing my experiences with people about being a former runaway street kid only really led to the automatic assumption that people could treat you lesser-than, and when you start noticing it more when people take advantage of it, it can lead to yet more confidence shattering experiences.

Many of the people that have experienced homelessness or are out on their own had no real choice but to develop hypersensitivities to manipulation and exploitation. It certainly has its critical benefits for those that choose to value them, but many of us simply must learn over time to be wiser and more careful in our ways of challenging such toxicities, because too often it can seem for no real reason that everything simply turns against us despite our best intentions, which brings about enough shock in itself.

Deep down people know we've got street-wisdom but when we try to use it our protests against ill behaviors and mistreatment are forever invalidated by the world around us, whilst those playing constant mental chess moves and play under the rules of black magic, always seem to get their way.

If we ever needed a revolution in how people treated each other as human beings and in a truly authentic way that wasn't just for show, then it was now. Not through Facebook, not through news articles, but through real-life down on the ground reactions to meaningful events. Despite the current status quo often leading it to putting a target on your head, it's still quite an extraordinary and empowering feeling to know that you've risen above the spell and decided that you were going to do what was right instead of easy. Few want to admit that they can easily fall under the spells woven by those manipulating the sense of group harmony, but most of us, even myself, can be prone to it all I think.

Just like the Irish and black folk back in the day, and just like any other person that's had to fight hard over time to be accepted and understood by other sections of society, at some point perhaps it's time for those like me to see our true value again, and refuse to be constantly tossed aside, beaten down, stitched up and cornered regular with no option but to try and fight our way out of it. Living within a society that nearly always denies that it happens leaves many of us jobless, with criminal records and in some cases the discrimination and abuse is left to rot for so long that tragedies and violent outcomes for the most exploited and neglected among us can become inevitable.

It's time for an essential shift in how those from backgrounds of homelessness are seen and valued by society. It's no good for society's vulnerable to be merely posterchildren for those that may be in denial of exploitation but put more energy into their homeless charity websites and fundraising projects. Nor should the concept of helping and enabling such people to develop rich and meaningful lives be left to the charity sector at all.

The real change will come from a genuine sense of inclusion in the community on various levels, leading homeless people to become valued for their experiences and knowledge rather than mocked, judged, misunderstood, and taken advantage of by all sorts of different people around, including landlords and schemers involved in government funding plots.

We've had enough of our experiences and feelings being invalidated and being told that we're not worthy enough to receive the same responses and treatments that others seem to get. Significant amounts of people from the care system are feeling too isolated and these are real lives that we're talking about. Something simply has to change.

We're not here to be labelled as crazy or psychotic just for expressing our injustices, or simply caring and feeling let down with the door too often being slammed shut on us.

And we're not here to believe that we're only worth what so many people want us to believe. Not always through words, but through actions or more importantly the lack of them.

We do matter!

#UnderdogsRising

Chapter Two – A little about me

For those of you that don't already know much about me, here's a bit of an introduction.

Firstly, I was an eighties child born and raised in the West Midlands, UK, for half of my childhood at least anyway.

Those that have read *Poems From a Runaway* will know that I didn't have a relationship with my dad from the age of around four, and wouldn't see him again until I was thirteen years old. The reunion had happened due to a chance encounter after nan from his side had recognised my face and name in one of the local newspapers when I'd been missing in London at twelve years old.

Before that though, by the age of eight I was already asking my mum questions about him, in which in the years leading up to me trying to find him by phoning people in the phone book with the same name, she'd explained to me a bit more about his story.

Before the search for my dad had been floating around in my mind though - I was a passionate footballer as a young kid, soccer for those living on the other side of the pond. Like a lot of us back then we were playing it outside for every single minute that we could until it had got too dark to see the ball, or when the last of us could hear the jungle-calls of our mums calling us back in from several streets away.

Being a young kid, I never particularly liked the pointless fighting that I often felt I had little choice but to partake in on the street. It was something that would happen a lot in the small town of Rugeley, especially in a place that had lost its buzz over a decade beforehand once the pits had closed down and employment opportunities were lessened. I'd often find myself baffled by the repeating circumstance of two lads walking past me, then one jogging back towards me – "Oi mate, mate, my friend says will you fight him?" Even back in those days I was like "Ay? What?"

But it was just that sort of town with that sort of vibe at the time, and when trouble came to the house I was taught quickly of my two options. Go back inside and risk it keep happening again, or go outside and fight the kids that were waiting for me and hope that it all went away afterwards.

Not that I ever really understood it though - parents and kids in circles shouting at one kid to hit the other is something that I still hang my head in shame about today, I just don't think that it's right, but for some people it's a genuine attempt to find a way to teach their kids not to be pushovers.

My mum's advice on the potential longer-term outcomes had been right to much a degree, and conflict with certain individuals or pairs often would soon go away afterwards. Still though, despite my mum's best intentions and sharing how she'd got through her own experiences - I never did feel in the end that it truly set me up right for dealing with such conflict in the adult world, where often much trickier power games can be at play.

Although I'm certainly not advocating violence at all, sometimes I feel that things would be a lot easier for people like myself if it was punches that we could see coming towards us instead of the vicious

Machiavellian and psychopathic mind games that can be so often at play.

As you might have already noticed - home life wasn't exactly harmonious at some point, and at the age of ten I'd been frequently running away and going missing for weeks on end, which eventually led to much longer periods of time missing in places much further away from home.

In those first days roaming across Staffordshire and the Midlands - I'd make my way down main roads in the middle of night whilst walking from town to town before eventually getting picked up by the police, or flagging them down as they were driving past once I'd become completely exhausted a few weeks later.

A few people comment nowadays that I must have been scared back then, and although there were indeed a few highly anxious moments here and there, for most-part the fearlessness I had was out of naivety more than anything, and a lack of understanding of people and the real dangers of the world.

It's perhaps one reason why I'd go on to notice through my friend Joanne that the sex workers on the backstreets of Brick Lane, and also Joanne herself, had in many ways seemed to be among those naturally protective over myself and other runaways that they'd find roaming the city streets, as they themselves knew all too well what it was like to learn the hard way of some of society's ugliest and darkest manifestations.

Going into foster care had seemed to settle me down for a little while, but the pattern had soon broken once I'd been moved from my second foster home that I'd actually been quite happy and stable at, living with a couple called Hazel and Gordon. I'd arrived one day from school when they looked at me with a sorrowful look and told me that we all needed a chat. Social services had phoned them earlier on that day and said that I was going to be moving to a new permanent foster placement first thing in the morning.

I was only supposed to be with Hazel and Gordon as a short-term solution until longer term foster parents became available. They'd most likely felt bad by now for suggesting a few weeks prior that instead of moving to a new home - that instead they fostered me long term, which I was all for at the time. I suppose upon finding out that I was moving on such short notice I would have protested it more at the time if I hadn't have felt so powerless about the decisions being made about my life, being only ten years old.

After moving onto my next foster home that had their own family of young children, being the only foster child among them had caused me to feel like the outsider there in many ways. It was the feeling of being an infiltrator almost, and I remember clearly the feeling that I was getting right in the middle of someone else's natural family unit. I'd felt like a young person that had just landed there from another planet almost, and was somebody that nobody really knew very well apart from on paper, not like they all knew each other anyway.

At the age of around twelve, and on a day that I'd been suspended from school for getting into a fight with a lad that had been trying to bully me in class, I'd decided to run away again on the spur of the moment, stealing ninety pounds from the mantlepiece at my foster home that was meant for the Providence man I think.

I'd never seen ninety pounds and in such easy reach before, and had convinced myself that it was enough for me to start a new life somewhere. Later that day and several train-hops across various cities I'd found myself a hundred and thirty miles away in London for the first time ever.

I'd been missing for around six weeks when I first ran away there, but after eventually getting caught one day and taken back home I'd soon return to the east end where I started to know people, including my newfound friend Joanne, and my future stints going missing would often go on to be for many more months at a time.

Not too long before I'd turned thirteen, and soon after going missing and back to London again, at some point I'd found myself out on my own after arriving back in Whitechapel to find that Joanne had been put into a secure unit whilst I'd been back in the midlands.

Needing to get food, I returned to the soup kitchen just off Brick Lane, in which I'd tell them as usual that I was around eighteen years old so that I could get in without anybody reporting me to the police. One day I'd been befriended there by a guy that had seemed concerned about me being out on the streets, and had offered me a place to stay in his flat. Although I'd politely and thankfully refused after him offering the first few times, eventually after numerous more offers I think that the idea had certainly got into my head, and at the time I felt that I could have done with the rest anyway having been sleeping out in doorways.

What I'd presumed was a kind and friendly offer had led me to being exploited into selling fake porn video cassettes on Petticoat Lane market, which I knew were completely blank. Upon returning with him to his flat in Edmonton Green and a few days later being asked for money from him, he'd held up with a machete and stolen my things, where I eventually escaped sprinting as fast as I could to the train station.

After changing trains a couple of times and heading into central London, I eventually found myself in Victoria where I'd go on to spend my thirteenth birthday sleeping rough on the Apollo Theatre steps and often using the nearby internet cafe that had just opened across the road.

Not too long after that I'd get caught begging by the police on the steps to the entrance to Victoria underground station, and after being taken back up to the midlands by the authorities again I'd soon be back in London within a week or two, where I'd eventually go on to find a big doorway on Piccadilly that had become my own spot for a couple of years.

For significant parts of my younger teenage homeless experience, my days had been spent exploring London's many different places and sights. Despite the obvious concerns and dangers that runaway children can face out on the streets - it's fair to say that despite my story still having its own tragedies, I was one of the luckier ones.

For me, looking back at it didn't feel like complete doom and gloom, which is something I think society can often struggle to understand and undervalue quite often. The concept of people having to adapt and try to learn to be happy in the circumstances that they find themselves in can too often be dismissed or be off-putting and confusing to some people. But the disrespectful and shameful tones are easier thought and said when the boot is on the other foot.

It's fair to say that like many other people of similar life experiences, I was indeed much happier and content with my life before I'd known otherwise. I do believe though that a person can move on and build from such past experiences without having to feel ashamed about it, and if anything, find themselves valued and appreciated for the street-wisdom that they've learned along the way.

As for reflecting on my childhood and adolescence as a runaway, it only brings me more questions than answers when I think back about how the authorities knew where I was on Piccadilly by a certain point. Police officers that had already taken me in before were simply walking past me as if they hadn't even seen me, leading to both confusion and relief after getting the usual butterflies and preparing myself to be taken in and sent back to the midlands.

But I'd become surprised when nothing often would happen in the end. I always had a blag, a fake identity and many of the details ready for when the police officers that had never seen me before that would come and stop me. But it was different when I saw the ones that already knew me for being a runaway. Maybe they just knew that if they went to all of the effort to take me in that I'd be back down there again few days later anyway.

It's something that I've been thinking a lot about recently, and it's possible that it was their way of trying to protect me from getting skittish again and disappearing off into unknown areas. Perhaps they'd figured that I was coping with it all ok out there to some degree with it being safer on Piccadilly than Whitechapel. Maybe they didn't care though, it was just easier for them to leave me to it. An inconvenience perhaps? Who knows?

With being only the other side of the park from Buckingham palace though, I'd be surprised if I wasn't at least checked out by the anti-terrorism units or royal security at some point. Not that I know the real workings of such security operations.

It's something that I ponder on from time to time though, wondering if they ever looked at any of the street homeless as potential threats to the local upper-elites living and roaming around Green Park and Mayfair, or if they'd simply just ignored us.

After yo-yo'ing between the streets and usually either children's homes or foster care as well as a brief stint in a secure unit and young offenders, at the age of sixteen I returned back to my hometown of Rugeley in Staffordshire, but as usual not for long.

I was back on the streets again initially, but this time being sixteen I was now officially an adult. But I'd soon had enough of begging on the side of the road and sleeping in doorways once I'd started noticing others my own age walking past me and enjoying a seemingly normal life out with their peers. That's when I decided to own up about my age to the homeless day centre that I'd been going to for two years.

Now I was sixteen and could access the same sort of help that I'd had to abandon before due to being a missing teenager that was masquerading as an adult, and had been unable to take those opportunities of help given to me at the time. But now things were different, and I'd go on to ask the workers in the day centre if they could help me get anywhere to stay, stressing that I felt my life living on the streets and in doorways had now ran it's course, and I just wanted to feel like a normal person again.

The staff there were quite supportive in fact, claiming that they'd had their slight suspicions that I may have indeed been a runaway. By the end of the day they helped me get a room in a homeless person's hostel just down the road, before I was eventually taken in by a group of squatters, and for a number of years I'd go on to live in warehouses, abandoned churches and old factories among other places where we'd put on raves at the weekend - which back in those days would often have a somewhat bright mix of London's semi-legal entrepreneurs, goa heads, and young Latin Americans, Europeans and Brazilians that had all contributed to one of London's secret weekend communities.

They were good times for most part, but it would be fair to say that even back then exploitative elements had existed in my life which meant I was put in a few situations that I wasn't exactly happy with. Still though, like many arriving on the scene back then, these pulsating underground worlds hidden away in the deep pockets of London had felt so new to many of us that it had brought some sort of euphoric and almost church-like revolutionary excitement about it.

There were a lot of elements within it all that I wouldn't change for the world, and some that I wish I could have experienced with a bit more peace and wisdom about me. What it did do though was give someone like me, a former runaway kid, the chance to mingle and feel appreciated outside of the homeless community, which was generally never the case beforehand. Being able to embrace that acceptance and feeling of intimacy can be a huge thing for someone like me that until those points in life had only generally been welcomed and accepted on natural levels by other people on the streets and in similar situations, or those helping us. Entering such worlds can subconsciously bring about many questions such as "am I even welcome here?" or "do they trust or respect me?"

See, despite having no problem whatsoever at the time connecting with people in the somewhat 'street' world that I'd been living in beforehand, where for me any trust, closeness and intimacy was often sacrificed in the name of robust defence, unlike a lot of the people that I'd go on to be partying with, for me even simply being in a room full of people and feeling that were truly accepting of me had at times felt quite overwhelming. Despite some of the psychedelic-induced experiences certainly making some of those inner journeys a lot more vivid for me, I think what it was actually doing was peeling off the mask that I'd wear to reveal more clearly those trust and intimacy issues within myself.

Being in such states had forced me to face the side effects of my lack of strong and consistent day-to-day connection with people in normal situations, which is likely the reason why I talk, write and sing so much about it all because of the number of times I've felt the lack of it.

Many people would easily presume me as a wreck-head upon hearing about my past with the squat parties, and I've even been laughed at when I've gone on to tell one or two people that I consider a lot of it valuable work experience being a young person back then.

It gets sneered at by some people mainly because they've got their own preconceptions of other people's lives, but for me knowing that at sixteen years old I was helping to run the bars, assisting on the doors and generally helping out the rest of the crew with whatever I could, I can pat myself on the back somewhat for being known to be reliable among my circle of friends at least, even if people that don't know me well do prefer to believe that I'm some useless bloke from the streets with little skill or use to him.

Perhaps this is the first time that I've spoken in public about such anxieties, which I was never really sure if it was always obvious to most people or not. 'Why would they trust a street kid?' I thought, and – 'do they think that I'm dodgy?' were often some of the things that would cross my mind for a while whilst meeting people at the parties.

It's fair to say that I got shown a fair bit of love by some of the people that I'd met. Still though, a part of me wishes that the now older and slightly wiser me could go back to those times to fully enjoy the experience without all the inner anxieties, but everything happens for a reason I suppose.

After a couple of years or so, our times putting on the squat parties came to an end, and I'd reaffirmed to myself my love in busking. Although I'd busked with a guitar for a few months whilst on Piccadilly as a runaway kid, and a few times whilst living at the hostel in Vauxhall, I'd started to take it more seriously, doing the best that I could to separate any sort of 'homeless street vibe' from it, which at times was unavoidable and not through any lack of trying.

Busking wasn't always an easy income, but for a while it was a beautiful life. I met some great people whilst out there in the city streets and in towns across the country. Both the towns and the cities brought their own energies in which new friends were made as well as short-lived and in the spur of the moment intercontinental flings, as well as newfound friendships with fellow musicians and other people that I'd met along the way. Those were some good times as it goes, and what I think your twenties are supposed to be for. Well, that's what I've convinced myself anyway.

Busking in the evenings in London was often a great vibe whether I'd been deep inside the tunnels of the underground performing to the passing commuters, or if I'd been elsewhere outside on the busy city streets.

It had been my only income for a few years where I hadn't even been getting benefits, and having completely dropped out of the system to much a degree I was just trying to make something work I suppose. I loved what I did though, and I think everybody could see that, so in many ways despite not earning much money at all, in other ways I was living the dream.

Mostly, I was just making it up as I went along, winging it whilst learning about life from the world around me and my squatter friends who were all creatives, artists or hustlers in their own ways.

Perhaps it was just the energy of London back then, or the sense of change in the air - but life was always somehow bringing me to protests and demonstrations. Often, I'd end up at one simply by chance as if the energies had been drawing me there, and often with my guitar with me having been on my way busking.

I certainly didn't do the best of keeping my head down whilst at the protests though, and admittedly I'd go on to learn of how all too easy it can be to get sucked in and immersed into the chaos of a large demonstration when things between the police and demonstrators are getting heated up. It brings up some memories that I'm certainly not proud of, in which these days I reflect much differently on, and which shows how hindsight can be an important thing when it comes to young people ending up in the middle of the dramatic conflict of such events.

Sometimes I wonder how much effect it has on my life and prospects being one of the many people that has a history of protest and activism. Despite later on down the line being told by police officers at anti-war protests down in Brighton that they knew I wasn't the type to cause any trouble, still I can't help but wonder sometimes if I was on public order intelligence databases perhaps containing video clips of me in my younger years, and whilst caught in heated moments, giving the appearance to authorities as being somewhat of a loose cannon.

Hopefully those a little more understanding of human nature can cut me a bit of slack with that one, because the subject of young people getting wrapped up in crowd and mob-mentality and the psychology behind it is rarely spoken about despite its extreme relevance in today's era.

Several years later, life in London had felt a little freaky, with me starting to get stopped and searched all the time and constantly moved on from my busking spots. It was often hard to tell whether these things were repercussions to ending up on the front line of demonstrations, or if it was just natural changes in policing dynamics in London.

A lot of other things were going on too though, which despite the urge to hold back talking about them because people might think I sound a little crazy, I know that public knowledge will always catch up with me, so I'll be writing about them in this book. Things felt so bizarre that one event had led me to packing my things into a suitcase and leaving London for Brighton at five o'clock in the morning, despite only having been there once ever before on a day trip out.

Perhaps this is an important time to mention that I was also in the middle of prosecuting the police for perverting the course of justice, which I go into later on in this book.

Life wasn't all about busking and being a complete drop out to the system though, and I'd gone through a number of legitimate jobs here and there. In my earlier twenties there was one in particular that I enjoyed and I could have stayed on it if I hadn't yet again had been completely stitched up.

Moving to Brighton though had certainly been an eventful few years, and for those that don't know it and might need a description - it's a very vibrant and welcoming party town. Perhaps even the Los Angeles or California of the UK to some degree, and as I'd soon come to find out - certainly not the cheapest area of the country to live in, but still a great experience to be there for a while that I'd recommend anyone to do at some point.

It's where I'd made the first ever batch of my handcrafted beads, but even more importantly it's where I had my first (and currently only) child, my lovely daughter. Although I keep her name out of a lot of my work, she's certainly been the reason for me still being here in my darkest moments that's for sure, and the proud dad moments that make it all worth it.

Having leaving London after a series of very strange events, I arrived down in Brighton and had been taken in for a short while by a friend that I'd only known from online social media before getting there. My attempts to keep my head down and stay under the radar had soon come to an end though, as she was a supporter and regular demonstrator with a local anti-war activist group that would protest every week outside a factory that had made weapons parts.

According to the activists there at the time, the parts were to be used in aircraft in the Israeli and Palestinian conflict over in Gaza from what I'd been hearing. Despite coming to find that Brighton was a place with a lot going on, I'd been trying to stay low-key upon first getting there, but within a couple of weeks I'd got to know too many people to simply blend in.

Places such as Brighton had been a magnet for those like me that were searching for other free spirits and roamers of the earth. A few of those that I'd met remained in the city, but equally many moved on to the next chapters of their lives after enjoying the experience of such a vibrant place.

Brighton was certainly a city that I'd fell in love with, it had everything I stood for – booming with liberalism, environmentalists, unique characters, artists, musicians, creatives, graffiti artists as well as being an LGBT stronghold. Brighton gave me the opportunity to actually iron out some of those 'hope you don't think I'm gay mate' anxieties, which tends to be something that disappears the more people you connect with.

Perhaps I'm getting way too deep into this now, but with this book being about prejudice and stigma I believe it's healthy for each of us to acknowledge and accept our own failings at connecting with, or understanding certain demographics of people.

A lot of folk, myself included, don't even realise when they're treating somebody a little differently simply because of a thought, anxiety or a preconception that they've had in their head. Perhaps these thoughts shed a light on how those working with young people that seem to be displaying strong homophobic tendencies might want to think about the idea of getting them to meet a person that they highly respected, yet didn't know they were gay. Such conversations such as the "Well did you know that I was gay?" can be quite powerful regarding the personal development of a person I believe.

Back then, I guess I was a bit more of a free-spirit and social butterfly than I am these days having gone though some significant life events. Brighton was also where I'd ended up in a betting shop one day whilst keeping out of an unexpected sudden rainstorm and inserting around three pounds into the roulette machine so that I wasn't simply hanging around, and eventually won over five hundred pounds over the space of an hour or two. Many might consider that extremely lucky, but it had immediately led to a chronic gambling addiction for a number of years, in which I went on to research deeper about and had set up the Neuroliberation Campaign to raise awareness of how the changes in gambling laws along with gambling addictions was affecting many individuals and communities.

Unfortunately though, after becoming mad enough at the industry to not gamble again, my addiction resurfaced a number of times, both when finding out that my dad had been diagnosed with cancer and also during a time I'd been convinced to set up a youth campaign about it and do talks in schools, but I'd completely pulled the plug on all of it due to some serious child protection concerns that I'd been fortunate enough not to allow to manifest. Even though the things I'd been going through were no excuse to go back to the bookies, for me at the time it was my heroin, my escapism.

I'd seen it as a coping mechanism to much a degree, the hypnotic effect of the electronic roulette wheel become a form of escapism from some quite dire and dangerous situations that I'd felt completely trapped in, often through no fault of my own. Thankfully I banned myself from the ability to gamble on any UK online sites a few years ago now through sites such as GAMBAN and GAMBLOCK which have been vital in ensuring that I wasn't tempted to 'have a flutter' online.

Just like an alcoholic, often just having that one drink can lead to months of devastation if I was to let it go that far.

I thought that I was invincible before all of that, but it's perhaps why I tell people that I can be a heroin addict without the heroin. Perhaps more of us should admit when we have addictions, even if they're more socially acceptable ones. When it comes to the black magic and dark sorcery of gambling, which consists of years of researching how to manipulate the human brain, the whole message of the campaign was how easily susceptible anybody can be to such neurological trickery.

Sure, on some level there is choice, but on another level things are so deeply rooted into our brains that even when we know something isn't good for us many of us will continue doing it anyway regardless, yet not always understanding exactly the real reasons why.

Unsurprisingly, the chronicity of the gambling often only came about when I'd felt somewhat isolated and in the rockier and more unstable parts of my life. But it was in one of those particular rocky situations that I'd decided to write *Poems From a Runaway* in 2016 after writing one particular poem titled 'Free Drinks on Haymarket' which was a memoir from being thirteen years old.

As for the living situation throughout it all, the multi-occupancy houses that I'd been moving in and out of whilst writing the book had been a whole new story in itself, and regardless if there really were organised repercussions or not happening due to my claims of child grooming happening somewhere, they were intense and crazy living situations to say the least, and worse than any of the squats I'd ever lived in during my younger days.

Nevertheless, after making use of the few months peace that I'd found myself having at some point, and after what seemed a repeating and constant major blow to my living standards, I bumbled on through the barrage of crazy coincidences, baffling reactions and dodgy characters whom all but one seemed to have some sort of connection with the local police.

Still though, whilst finally having one place to myself for a short while I was able to concentrate on writing and trying to perfect *Poems From a*

Runaway. The literary agents I'd contacted had wished me luck, but all said that it was too niche, which has taken me until now to fully understand that from a financial perspective they were right.

But I knew my chaotic life would mean it had been yet another half-complete and unfinished project of mine, and if I didn't just hammer on I'd just be wasting my time. And so, I finished the book before self-publishing it on Amazon as well as creating two other versions from book printers which had all been made possible by the generosity of those responding to my calls for support through a crowdfunding campaign.

The book wouldn't have even been released when I first said it would have without a few people that I'd met pulling together towards the end after a few unexpected twists and turns that had created some real intense pressure and mishaps out of my control. So once all the drama subsided and things had been positive again, with the book finally complete and now published it was time to start promoting it.

I'd seriously overestimated how many people that I knew would be interested in the book though. I guess you can't expect everyone to want to hear your story even with its central London landmark novelties, but over time I'd slowly come to start finding a new tribe so to speak, as well as reuniting with a few souls that I'd not seen since my younger parts of childhood.

The initial forty-something pre-orders that I'd sold was a decent result in the end, but I knew there was a lot more potential for the book than that, and so I went all-out building up email databases that I'd scraped from caffeine-fuelled google searches, sending out emails to thousands of people and organisations , which had consisted of press releases with statements from myself as if someone was interviewing me. Nobody really was at first, but this was my initial attempt at playing the hype game I suppose.

After researching the best ways on how to promote the book, it seemed best I started a Twitter account which has been a bit of a journey in itself. Things went quite well at first, but then as soon as I entered the world of trying to talk about child abuse things immediately went very silent, very quickly. Despite my social media activity these days often feeling as if I'm in my own echo chamber, I'd met some great people through it too. Most of those people include a whole scene of care leavers and support workers, many of which were and still are dedicated to making much needed improvements to the care system, as well as campaigning for better outcomes for care leavers.

Thankfully the email blasts didn't go completely un-noticed either. As well as the charity 'Missing People' getting back in touch with me and offering to feature me in some blogs and online interviews, so did a couple of other bloggers, social workers and fostering organisations too - which I'm truly grateful for when I think about it all, despite sometimes forgetting some of the great people that have helped to make a significant impact on getting *Poems From a Runaway* seen by more people. Despite the stresses that came with having to do everything on the extreme side of the breadline whilst funding a life-long tobacco addiction, it had been an overall enjoyable experience having met some brilliant people at events that I'd been to, some of which I'm still in touch with today.

Few really knew the intense situations that I'd been living in at the time whilst also trying to fight my way out of it all though. During the first few years of the book journey I'd been desperately trying to get out of the dodgy shared houses that I'd found myself in which had been proving to be more difficult than expected.

I think in many ways the exterior signs of my wear and tear of all of that might have hampered people's impression of me, the poor diet because of the kitchen items forever getting stolen and looking a little worn and thin with beady tired eyes, which is apparent in some of the photos from events over the years.

Another positive though, was that the journey had brought me close to a network of care leavers spread across the country that I feel privileged to have met because many of those people understand me a lot better than some others ever could.

Fortunately, things aren't as dodgy and chaotic these days. Perhaps being a little more comfortable in my living environment has allowed me the space to think more about a few things, and come to the realisation about how stigmas and discriminations still play out in my life today. The people presuming I'm not capable or wondering what on earth a person like me could know or have to offer, I still see as clear as day.

Who knows where life has taken me by the time I've finished this book? Hopefully challenging the subtle underbelly of stigma and discrimination with a lot more force and surety now that I've been able to process much of it. I should of being challenging it a long time ago anyway, but when in many environments the numbers are against you, people can go years not being completely sure if they were in the right for standing up for themselves when the world responds by telling them to 'put up and shut up.'

As I know all too well these days, challenging the status quo can often be the quickest way to lose a job, or even friends – but that doesn't make it wrong to do, especially in an era where some are focusing their attention on ridding current cultures of their hate, venom, toxicity, systemic abuse and failings.

The vision is for people not having to be forced into unwinnable games, but for that it takes more people in society to choose firmly not to condone them, which is made a difficult task by being so deeply engrained into parts of our culture and human behaviour. When all of this stuff seeps into the world of employment then it's important for those in influential and managerial professional roles to keep their eyes open to those power battles that not only play out on higher levels, but equally happen often silently on ground level which can completely poison and falsify the depths of a work environment.

Ignoring it may seem the easy option, but I've seen too many managers that stand by that ethos not realise themselves how differently some people can talk about them when they're not around, and how that can immediately change once upon direct interaction. This might be the status quo in a few places of employment but it feels far from a healthy or progressive work team culture in my own opinion.

For all the talk of equal rights and the ridding of discrimination here in the UK, still there's a lot of work to be done around bringing awareness on a much deeper and practical level if we're going to create social and work cultures where people from all walks of life can genuinely thrive.

With no discredit to the fantastic work and efforts currently being undertaken by people to create change around stigma, unfortunately in today's climate of fast-paced content and short attention spans created through the sheer amount of content that we process, in many ways our current forms of education around stigmas and discrimination are all too often on a vague, superficial or diluted level.

That's not to say that the surface-skimming is intentional, but more of a fact perhaps of what the fragmented world of internet information sharing has become. The forms of marketing and communication that we often find ourselves digesting these days can leave many people thinking that the only discrimination people face are in such situations as being called names, or more visible events. In reality it is so much more than that, in which it can affect many aspects of a person's life, and if they struggle to cope whilst battling through it all then it can completely shatter a person's confidence in regard to future prospects or feeling welcomed into any community or workplace.

Until such discrimination is more deeply understood and acknowledged, then many of those going through it will simply continue to find themselves getting shut down by decision-makers upon standing their ground or bringing such issues to light in a natural call for resolution. Despite the attitudes that presume such a person will remain trapped having no other options, many will simply up and leave such an environment and search for a healthier way of daily living, which can be a silent misfortune for many businesses that might have lost decent workers because of such dynamics.

So, for those still reading this, I hope it can bring a little more insight into some of the unspoken elements of discrimination, mental health, homelessness and how the world sometimes interacts with all three.

Chapter Three – Acknowledging that the stigma is very real.

"I'm alright Jack."

I think it takes a person having gone through certain life journeys to truly understand what true discrimination can feel like, or even to know and recognise what it actually is. Even those like me that have gone through it can still go decades without really understanding it, despite it being right under our noses and constantly in our lives.

It can be difficult to express it to others when you do recognise it too, where attempts to highlight it can all too often be met with a sort of baffled or stunned reaction in which two different understandings of the world collide. Such a person will often leave such an environment scapegoated as the drama queen, chaos magnet or whatever labels people tend to reach for to plaster over the fact that things were easy enough before these so-called troublemakers started highlighting the often-exploitative abuse and injustices.

Care leavers like myself seriously need to start calling this stuff out more and challenge the lust for control which tends to get pushed onto some of us. What can start off as a person not even realising that they are treating a person lesser-than can all too often manifest into sabotage and exploitation. In that regard, paying off the mortgage and having a nice car and picket fence accounts for very little if one hasn't achieved the same success in the spiritual world, and we can all find ourselves growing in a variety of ways and have something that we can all teach other.

Plenty of people that might understand this often try their best to blend in, but for some people that's easier said than done whether that be because of background, race, alternative appearance, disability or any of other forms of stigma. Despite all of those currently raising awareness of discrimination in the world, too often the very people still going through it are often told through various forms of interactions and outcomes that they shouldn't have the right to stand up and speak out against it or demand better than the current standards. This book isn't just about the emotions, thoughts and feelings of those going through frequent discriminations - but how it has massive impacts on people's day-to-day lives and ability to get by, feel they belong and progress in the world.

Even those among us that can appear super-confident to the world can easily be misunderstood when that social confidence seems to count for nothing when such people reach out to the world around to tackle injustice, and nobody seems to bat an eyelid. Often at best when challenging what can be the status quo in some environments they'll be met with eyes that blatantly tell them not to rock the boat and that it's just not what we do here.

Over in the digital online world the popularity of certain advocates might have you believe that such stigmatized people now finally have a voice and the support of the world around them, but in an all too superficial world that doesn't account for the many more people still in the midst of their struggles, or simply buried by the algorithm, appearances can be deceiving.

Whether having being conscious of it or not, going through such stigma for so much of your life can result in you being built a bit differently in the end, which despite its positives of being able to think outside of the box and bring about some original ideas to the world, still to market anything to people these days there needs to be an air of familiarity about you. Marketers will tell you no doubt that many of their strategies are to get people to feel that they almost know you, but how do those from lives like mine that are so outside of the norms achieve that when they're aware that people just don't always feel that familiarity in their stories, especially for those that consider themselves the lucky ones in regards to the worlds that they've experienced.

Busking has been one of the major positives in my life though which had helped me often break through those barriers with those around me. Whilst there singing and playing guitar people didn't know much about my life and it was just all about the music. I've met many great different sorts of people through it too, people are just a lot nicer around you when you're busking in which it reminds me of that same sort of unity that can be created at a rave. Music is a powerful thing for sure, and it's brought me much light in my life as it has to for many others on similar roads, I couldn't recommend enough getting instruments to those young people trying to find themselves in the world, and it might end up becoming a form of therapy and meditation for some. I couldn't even imagine who'd I'd be without it in all honesty.

Many people like myself go on to be low income entrepreneurs, which despite its struggles can give us the chance to get away from those worlds of seeing opportunities constantly taken away in front of our very eyes and doors closing in on us in what can be a confusing reality to function daily in for those that sense that the stigma has made them feel unworthy of being counted for by others in many different scenarios.

Those like myself often see today's sense of competitiveness in the work world too often completely skewed and self-defeating. The ever-growing ethos that those already in their job have to constantly work harder to prove themselves over others in order to keep it not only creates much 'disfunction in denial' and toxic dark-arts in the workplace, but it also means that no doubt with being played like a puppet on a string day in and day out then it's no wonder the levels of behaviour such as cohesive control, stalking and general manipulation seep into the family homes and social lives of many people.

Despite a past of being in care and having professionals write so much about our lives in places such as children's home you'd think that those circumstances could have been used to the advantage of those needing mental health support and care. But for too long it's been the case that many of those from backgrounds such as myself have been put the back of the queue and sort of seen as not worthy of the same level of support than others from more seemingly regular lives.

There's still hope for the though, and whilst in the process of writing this book it's been great to see the stigmas and discrimination that care leavers like myself can face finally being acknowledged by professionals and councils throughout the UK.

I suppose deep down I want to put a little more depth into those stigmas and discriminations that people can find themselves up against. You'd think in 2023 that with all the people going on about it that we're almost there, but merely scratching the surface and throwing out a few soundbites will do nothing really to change the workings of society to help tilt to the balance for those having gone through it in their lives.

Until stigma is understood and processed on that much deeper level than just soundbites and slogans then people such as myself will continue to find that fair and rational responses won't be in our lives as we continue to shake our heads and quote how we can't believe that all of this is all still happening in today's age.

For those that have tried to highlight either their own experiences of injustice or have selflessly tried to make a stand for others and have so far felt ignored and told by the world that caring simply wasn't worth it – hang in there, your head and your heart might be more needed than you think.

For what has been an extremely tough time for those failing to understand the more complex and twisted forms of human behaviour and abuse perhaps now is an interesting time where such issues have come to surface. Not through Youtubers jumping on fashionable topic trends or tinfoil hat conspiracy theorists, but if looked at carefully by others and taken inspiration from - perhaps the recent inquiry into the standards and systemic failings of the Met police can not only be used to review other police forces relating to such matters, but the UK workforce in general.

Despite its importance regarding incompetence, corruption and failings in the police, I think we would be foolish to think that this only happens in that environment, and might want to start wondering if such cultural behaviours could be happening in other industries that have previously managed to fly under the radar.

This could in fact turn out to be a full-scale review of not only the whole of Britain and beyond, but could challenge much deeper roots into both human behaviour and how we value and respect other humans and other life on earth. A grand awakening perhaps for those that see the value in it.

The realization of abuse scandals constantly surfacing thirty years too late is a clear sign that something much deeper rooted and established is at play here. Few people want to believe that they are bystanders of abuse or have completely shut down a whistleblower, yet for various reasons the intensity of the subject can often make a person shy away. Perhaps they were abused as a child? Maybe one of their relatives is a peadophile? Or maybe it's just too much to think about?

Going deeper into all of that though, the question 'where did we go wrong?' is too often merely something for headlines. How much deeper do such failings to make a real stand against abuse go in the world that we live in?

Perhaps some of the recent undercover reports about elderly care homes might give you the answer to that, but how many other industries too? As someone that has both been in care and someone that's also worked in a children's home in my adult life I can confirm that such failings do exist. I've seen first-hand how blatant bullying amongst young residents can be not only condoned but perhaps unintentionally encouraged by staff members. These failings really do go much deeper than the police force and are embedded deep within our very culture.

Relying on authority and media to teach us the way to be decent human beings just doesn't cut it anymore when such failings are shocking revelations of how society really functions and brushes its problems under the carpet.

The truth has always been within sight and earshot though, but perhaps people have felt too powerless until now. Who'd believe us over a seemingly well-respected and charitable member of the community?

But these things are changing, and I do believe something special is going on, perhaps the era of superficiality is soon to be gone, and people are starting to see the real impacts of it. Surely there's something in the soul that craves for something deeper than this? Something more real, true and wholesome?

Few would want to admit how much crime and desperation merely being a bystander helps to create. Perhaps not always on an individual level, but certainly on a collective one where those most lost and confused are beamed the message socially that they're out on their own with their struggles and that maybe the government will help them or something.

From abuse to homelessness, and also lets not forget about those that deem themselves untouchable through our lack of action, what really are the side effects of a philosophy that thinks that there's always someone else there to help.

I get that sometimes people simply don't know what to do, but when we're given the options - and one's based on love and unity instead of hate and division – perhaps both individually and collectively we should start taking those chances and supporting them more.

The domino-style knock-on effects of people failing to step in for the better good when they could have can often be overlooked, and with a world much more interconnected than we often give it credit for, the chances of it even coming back to bite you in the backside in one way or another are pretty reasonable. Perhaps nobody can be truly selfless if it's because they want a better world for themselves and those around them.

As for being a care leaver and a runaway, despite my struggles and the places that I've been it's fair to say that in many ways I was one of the lucky ones. Perhaps being able to play some guitar and sing a bit brought me not only the pounds and pennies that I'd needed during some of my more financially tough times - but had given me chance to meet some lovely people in what would have otherwise been an isolating and lonely experience whilst going through the majority of my adult struggles in life feeling almost completely alone.

Through the busking I was lucky to meet people with sensible heads
though too, which not everybody in such vulnerable positions have the
fortune of. Many go down roads that they never intended to, perhaps
the only doors that had ever opened for them at the time, and an easy
target to be exploited in numerous different ways.

I think generally the worse it gets for people and the more obvious
signs of wear and tear some of them have, then the less trust and
chances get offered to them in general which is no wonder why many
can go on to give up on living a seemingly regular life because before
somebody can go and get a job that simply doesn't exploit the shit out
of them then first they must be accepted in by the tribe and not be
exploited by those who deem it their right to do so.

Despite most people coming across some forms of exploitation or
other in life, there are still those that through no fault of their own may
struggle to fathom what it's truly like to go through its most dangerous
and damaging moments actually almost completely alone.

Obviously. it's an extremely important thing that people have family to
fall back on for advice, words of encouragement or practical help
when they most need it, and I'd certainly want that for my own
children too. But for all of the valid self-pride that some people can
take in being able to maintain stable patterns of work and
accommodation for the majority of their lives whilst looking down at
those with much different results, hopefully those people have realised
how truly lucky they really are to not be pushed away by their own.

What really did cause that hateful venom and undertones towards
those that have gone through life with generally less opportunity and
rights than themselves? I guess some are just desperately scared of

losing the security that they've got whilst failing to see that we could all just co-exist a little better in general.

Until you've experienced numerous times the tiring situation of being trapped in complex housing situations such as living in substandard accommodation, neglected homeless hostels ran by business people, or even being able to get any help at all then it's all too easy to say a person should just move on or keep trying.

There are many out there trying constantly but not all of them have age or ability on their side. Many get used to it, at least they're surviving which by that point it's the best outcome for a lot of people. I myself saw how despite finding it difficult to find work a lot of the time whilst homeless - one way or another I'd found a way to get by.

'Spongers' some people call them, but really many are just doing their best to survive another day.

Contrary to the treatment and reactions that many homeless people might come across it's not so much the case of people wanting to choose an easy life bouncing around out of a backpack – but more the case that the reality of being given phone numbers and places to go in hopes of accommodation or support often lead to nowhere, in which many homeless people themselves could tell you which support services that you presume are out there for them would only result in wasted efforts to their day.

It's all well and good saying that if somebody wanted the help enough then they'd try it. "I'd walk ten miles if I knew I'd get the help" some might say, but it's too easy to think that when your daily routine consists of getting the rest, food and security a person needs to function.

But if you're spending much of your life on your feet and moving around all day anyway, and generally not eating or sleeping well due to homelessness, then along with knowing deep down that the place you're about to go to for help will likely be a huge waste of time then can you really blame someone for taking the easier option and getting through the day? What else should they do? Pull their hair out?

It's taken me all of my life up until now to realise the real position that I found myself in as both a care leaver, former child runaway and someone that has experienced homelessness a fair bit during my adult life.

I myself plodded on, and despite not always been aware of the stigmas that it had brought towards me, I now realise what I'd been battling through a lot of my life. An established ethos that's been around for many hundreds of years that trickles down from the top that such people are merely vagrants and delinquents worthy of being exploited and abused.

Perhaps a widescale shift of perspective on homelessness has been a very long time coming because for how many centuries has ignoring important factors such as mental health, physical health, unfortunate circumstances and situations way beyond peoples control played a factor in the homeless being seen as failures and spongers by some?

I suppose it's easier for many of the haves to want the have-nots out of sight, less repairs to do on society in their eyes I suppose. Uncovering the real reasons of why many people find themselves homeless would reveal too much truth about society and it's failings, and so I presume it would be much more convenient for the establishment to want everybody presume that it's all just about drug addiction and mental health, when they are merely just some of the symptoms of the root causes that we should really be focusing on.

Being somebody that left care with a criminal record also brings me some much deeper questions about my life, especially when I see the history of how many of those from backgrounds like myself went on to have a relationship with crime and the authorities for many years.

That's no discredit to the many care leavers out there that went on to live more regular lives, but the one thing that I've noticed when it comes to the representation of people that grew up in the care system from professionals is that such people and outcomes are largely ignored or forgotten about. Considering around a quarter of prisoners in the UK were in the care system maybe this is something that needs to be acknowledged on a much deeper level too.

I suppose if constantly going missing across the country and evading the police from the age of ten hadn't somehow put me on the radar of the authorities, perhaps some of young-teen impulsive and irresponsible forms of 'protest' or mucking around hadn't helped either.

Not that my Yahoo chat handle would have done me much good either whilst inside what were then twenty-four hour internet cafes where I chatted online with people claiming I was an adult, with my username 'Smash_Up_The_Government.' It would be fair to assume that behind the username was perhaps a dedicated activist disgruntled with the authorities, but in truth it was a fourteen year old street kid that had taken inspiration from a political comedic song from the website a group called Cyderdelic from a BBC-Three spoof documentary subtitled 'The Revolution Will Be Televised'.

I suppose it's taken me until now to realise that it's no wonder that the police had been filming me all throughout the first ever mass demonstration that I'd found myself at in Central London back then. After being arrested on my way home from the demo for alarm, harass and distress for saying "why the fuck are you treating me like a piece of shit?" to a policeman that had been breathing down my neck whilst I'd been sat on my own having a rest on Whitehall, I'd come to find around a month later after being taken by two quite friendly CID that had come with a warrant for my arrest one morning that the police had put together a video tape which had consisted of numerous clips of me throughout the demonstration right from the very start of it when I'd first arrived there with my friend from the hostel, Phil.

I'd been surprised by the amount of footage that had been captured and put on the tape which has taken me two decades to get my head around because despite my foolish stunts before the age of sixteen and my reading of anti-capitalist literature online - I'd never really been involved with any sort of political movements or anything before. I was just a young homeless lad that for a few years had been living locally on the streets as a runaway and during that time in a hostel in Vauxhall.

Maybe those foolish stunts prior to being there had already put me on the radar of the authorities too though, and considering I'd arrived at that demonstration with my late friend Phil who'd been given a jumpsuit from someone he'd known from the campaigner group 'The Wombles' , then quite possibly that fact alone may have meant that through association I was looked into at the very least.

Ironically my late friend Phil eventually ended up gravitating towards different directions of the political spectrum, when around fifteen years later he'd be finding himself involved in some of the English Defence League protests. Before that I'd become good friends with Phil and his then girlfriend Trixie for a while when I was sixteen and all three of us were living in the homeless hostel across the road from Vauxhall bridge. Despite life taking us on our own paths and different directions, me and phil would often bump into each other in random places throughout the country every few years and had got back in touch for a while a few times.

Despite his involvement in some of EDL protests I knew that Phil was far from a racist though. Misguided at times perhaps, yes, but I'd seen the way he naturally interacted with people of all nationalities throughout London to just know that it wasn't why he was there, and through deeper conversations he'd expressed that a large part of being at the EDL protests was for the intense energy and the chaos of the tussles with the police. Not that he was ever particular hateful towards anyone or an aggressive type even, in which he'd admitted in one of our conversations that much of it was just about letting off some steam.

Even though politically we'd branched off into different directions it was something that neither of us had ever let get in the way of our friendship. I'm guessing that some of those from either side of the political spectrum would frown upon it I guess, but both of us knew that we had much more in common than our differences, especially with our pasts of being in care and on the streets as young teenagers.

But those conversations that we'd had not too long before Phil's tragic and unfortunate passing had also made me think about much deeper things that for many years have been not quite a full-blown paranoia, but perhaps a constant on-and-off wondering if parts of my life or even all of it had in any way been influenced by the more shadowy side of political policing, the deep state.

As for what had made me ask those questions though back then in my early twenties when life in London had felt quite strange for a while, the things I'd done at around sixteen years old had been merely deeply buried memories at the time. Not that I helped myself much though. As well as being a naïve and unguided wannabe anti-war activist at the time, perhaps with claiming on Myspace to want to organize demonstrations - the authorities might have actually needed to disrupt what I was doing because I'd be naïve to think that I could have made sure that everything was in place regarding crowd safety back in those days.

The thing is though, it makes me wonder what's really going on in society with other people with pasts similar to mine, because I know that I'm certainly not a unique case. For how long exactly have the authorities and mysterious agencies been keeping tabs or in some way influencing people such as myself that may have been deemed as the wild ones needing to be tamed, the unpredictable and unprogrammed. Decades? Centuries?

For hundreds if not thousands of years there's been a devalued and degraded homeless population that in many ways were seen as the criminal class, and in a similar fashion to slaves. A few of us might have had ancestors that had been on the same sort of lists that people might find themselves on in this very day and age. Perhaps those people out there that the authorities might deem needing to be tamed or controlled are in many ways devalued by proxy through the very nature of such covert manipulation, depending on its scale and depths.

I've no doubt that such programmes do exist, but in all honesty in today's world it's hard to tell the difference between what originates from professional realms and what is just people using modern forms of technology in an attempt to monitor and control others. More on all of that later though.

However, whilst also having to acknowledge my own failings and mistakes, the ever-repeating pattern of being completely stitched up and feeling like my own responses are hitting thin air leads to me wonder every now and then how deep the stigma and devaluing really goes.

Sometimes it really can all feel like a conspiracy, but I think really what we are seeing is a concept of such covert treatment and outcasting of those like myself being across the board, which can be a lot to fathom for some when they are unaware of the real reasons why such things are happening and where it all originates from.

What can merely be someone with a personality disorder playing Machiavellian games can turn into a whole new world of anxiety for those that have had certain questionable experiences like myself. Some of which I still experience today in regards to weird things happening to my electronic communication devices, and often at the most specific of times that make an impact, and I gather by now that much of it is about keeping your mind occupied on trash.

Why this happens to some people and exactly where it's coming from I simply don't know, and despite knowing I'll sound crazy, it's something that I've personally going through for many years and wonder exactly how many other people have not spoken out in fear of being labelled as a tin-foil hat and paranoid psychotics.

Either way, people such as myself are saying that it's happening.

If it wasn't for the fact that I'd already experienced and witnessed being on the outside looking in before I'd became an outspoken campaigner then it would be fair to say much of the freakier stuff may have been from my own doing.

I'd felt invincible in my early twenties, and in many ways naïve to the real workings and consequences of the world. Perhaps it would have been wise to keep my head down after receiving the compensation from the Met police and seeing the officers that had tried to stitch me up finally expelled from the force after three years in and out of crown court and an internal misconduct hearing. But no, instead I'd used some of it to set up the Neuroliberation campaign which was highlighting the rise in gambling addiction due to the proliferation of betting shops in the UK, which had mostly all made a significant portion of their profits from fixed odds betting terminals.

I myself was one of the many people that had found themselves inside of a betting shop and surprisingly winning a significant amount of money whilst playing electronic roulette which went on to become a chronic addiction lasting several years. More on that later, but my re-occurring passion for justice and change along with my naivety about its consequences has certainly made me a few enemies despite the many more friends.

I guess no matter what background you come from, if you're someone like me then unfortunately you really are a threat to those that greatly benefit from the people around them keeping their heads down and saying nothing.

That's certainly not meant to put anyone off from doing the right thing and standing up when you know that somebody needs to, but if anything just some words of advice and guidance for those young justice seekers feeling as invincible about it all as I did. Just play the game a little more clever if you can I suppose before you've got a target on your head and you can't see where its coming from.

As for some of the other injustices that I'll cover in this book, what often keep these sorts of factors at play is the illusion of true ethics, professionalism and officiality, which in today's era seems to be completely breaking down and revealing uncomfortable truths.

Although we know that power-seeking, exploitative and manipulative personal disorders exist, it's almost like we've often completely rejected to acknowledge that some of the well-established businesses and organisations of this world have grown from the very same sort of Machiavellian virus which has ran rampant in the world of big business. Simply put, the infection can be found almost everywhere.

Chapter Four – Standing out in protest

Perhaps for some of us, some significant event or hundred shifts us into a mindset of often putting our foot down immediately when we see the toxicity pushed on to others. Often being the first or even only ones to say a thing can be an empowering feeling yet it's important to understand that not everybody respects that. Even if they pretend to.

Let me remind you, none of this is ever easy. Trying to help make real change I mean.

That's been my biggest problem I suppose, feeling afterwards that I was punching above my weight with some of my campaigns and projects, but sometimes campaigners just need patience and to wait for the world to catch up with what they're talking about.

Following the crowds never did me much good really anyway, and I soon got bored of some of the repetitive chants I'd hear at the protests I'd been going to. Whilst out there I'd keep seeing that the real message had sometimes lost its meaning, and any actual powerful statements relating to the anti-war protests had been overshadowed with the usual generic chants as well as tussles with the police.

Unlike the mass numbers gathering for some political causes - those that find themselves going into any topic relating to the dynamics of abuse and human interaction will generally find themselves in a different world unless they already have a following, and even then their supporters may mysteriously drop off the radar. Despite the platform given to victims and whistleblowers by a small number of well-meaning journalists, the sight of people looking to make pro-active change is too often replaced with either 'follow the mob' culture or a deafening silence - whether that be regarding abuse towards children, women or anyone else.

Despite the illusion that large numbers of views on live predator sting videos can give, those on the other side of the lens will likely know all too well how we see that our calls regarding the true scale of abuse and an urge to prevent it are generally rarely acknowledged at all.

For many people it becomes a forever echo-chamber, where frustrated and understandably damaged folk find themselves wondering why everyone's just simply observing whilst not helping to make a stand or contributing to what they consider important and progressive conversations. Still though, perhaps it takes for you to get just hurt and frustrated enough to get so numb that you simply become fearless of getting stuck in. Such a theory would seem to make sense, but it's just a shame that what makes it off-putting to some is that the driving energy can be perceived as psychotic.

Being able to pay the bills, keep food in the cupboards and have a little extra for a rainy day often keeps many people just comfortable enough to see it as counter-productive to uproot some of the toxic and unhealthy elements within an environment. How many of us remember being the new person in a workplace and being an observant bystander where we look back and just wish we'd said or done something when it had happened?

It's similar psychological pressure to being in a religious cult in some ways, where all of us want to presume that we're morally robust and would always do the right thing, but despite that - we sometimes don't. As far as some are concerned, as long as the money is still coming in and nothing has seemed to change then everything is working just fine.

Yet those that naturally stand against toxic and destructive dynamics in all of their forms will become an immediate target in a spiritual battle that often brews deep between the lines and on a whole different level.

Those that lack self-control over their lust for mindless power and manipulation seem to always get their way over spellbound employers, leading to millions of decent people simply finding other jobs or being out of work after seeing that the situation is so well-manipulated and engineered appearing as if almost effortlessly by those possessed by such dark forces.

Our economic system is often so fragile that few employers will even take the risk of uprooting toxic and damaging dynamics or even unhealthy individuals because losing one person with a certain skill can cause so much disruption.

It's perhaps seen as easier in the short-term for the one expressing their concerns to leave, not the Machiavellian arse-licker who engineers the game to be perceived as highly needed yet is completely fudging his work and fobbing off the blame to others, no, no no.

It's a situation that I can only imagine is happening all of the time, because although those that remain calm and hide it better have more of a chance of learning to put up with it - anyone outspoken about diminishing such toxic dynamics, even just for their own benefit, will find themselves a guaranteed target of a whole lot of games.

The sense of stability and security plays a heck of a lot into it, of which those like me didn't feel that we had much to lose for a while, and so choosing to do what your heart is telling you is all well and good when you're young and feeling invincible. But then you have kids or something.

"At some point some of us realise that our faith in the collective pulling together to genuinely remove any of the needless crap from a situation has all but diminished..."

Well, that's what I'd written when I'd been sidetracked from this book. Perhaps it was all meant to work out the way that it has or something. But lately there's been something in the air, a spiritual revolution so to speak, and a growing concept that everything I'd written in this book was reflected back to me and shown that people like us, we're really not alone. And the stuff they try to do to us – yes, often it's real.

But as for 'faith in the collective pulling together to remove any needless crap' – well, that faith certainly has not diminished. Don't lose hope, seriously. Big things going on in the realms, believe!

The paragraph had gone on to explain that how for no good reason it was easy to start feeling like a freak when you're standing up when nobody else around you is. None of the most genuine of people uprooting such issues want to be the trouble magnet or the superhero wannabe. They just want decent standards of human behaviour and to be able to get on with their lives without constantly battling sadism and toxicity.

For all of the headlines of abuse scandals, cover-ups and systematic neglect, it's not as if people haven't been trying to shout out about all of this stuff for years only to experience a complete reality-flip once the majority of people around them appear almost lifeless in response to their concerns, as if any thoughts, feelings and opinions from those with backgrounds such as myself simply aren't relevant.

Whether it's the impression that the kids in care were all naughty kids, or that anyone that has experienced homeless must be a fool or a self-inflicted drug addict, it can often feel at times like nobody really knows you.

I also feel greatly for those experiencing homelessness with any obvious and visible cognitive impairments or mental health issues too, because all too often the amount of people that are automatically presumed to be on drugs is phenomenal when people simply didn't bother to think and look past their own prejudices.

For those that both happen to be struggling and also have a slower pace of thinking or speech, this is something which I think gets casually misunderstood a lot of the time which wouldn't if the element of homelessness hadn't been involved. In the 'regular' world such people might have others looking out for them, but those with such disabilities as well as facing homelessness can find themselves at a higher risk of being deemed as weird, crazy and on some levels treated as a subhuman.

Of course, it's not everyone that judges in such a way, but it's enough of a percentage to know that there's certainly a systematic problem with societal disconnection leaving many people feeling misunderstood and voiceless. Despite being seen as a normal situation by some, for me it beams a needless lack of understanding of other peoples lives and the disregarding of what if people like myself are saying even has any relevance to their world at all.

A lot of people that find themselves falling out of the system eventually have it engrained into them in the end that they'll be misunderstood and undervalued which can become a default state. Ironically, people like myself get asked all of the time in new jobs if we're going to be able to handle the work or be ok lifting the weight, almost as if people actually choose to forget the lengths many people from lives like myself have to go to simply to survive.

You become to realise that there are some people that actually want to think that you're incapable of such things, and rather than be pleasantly surprised by what they see often they'll go into some sort of inner rage that you've rattled their belief system. Those people simply don't want to believe that the person they thought was a fool with no formal education could be or get as good as anything as them. With the currently perceptions and stigmas about those from backgrounds like myself being the way they are currently, I think a lot of people mistakenly find getting it wrong a little bit embarrassing if anything else, and that's why some of us are more prone to getting fobbed off or stitched up than others.

As for street homeless, there are of course some fantastic people doing some great things to keep the warmth and the spirit going for those out there on the streets that need it. But whilst a lot of us see the many different acts of charity posted on social media, it can be all too easy to forget that some areas are more fortunate than others, as well as seeing through some of the sugarcoated exploitation created by respectable-looking money machines.

Sometimes the lack of familiarity for many people makes it hard for them to think about the real ins-and-outs and day-to-day living of those with such turbulent lives which can often lead to various false impressions, and because largely the current homeless social voice is somewhat unheard there are a whole load of factors completely overlooked into what causes people to fall into such traps in the first place.

Sometimes you'll get the misplaced advocate for homelessness quoting how they found themselves with nowhere once for a few weeks and if they'd managed to get back on track so quickly then why couldn't everyone else? On the other hand, those finding themselves struggling over the longer term will find their recognition as just poster boys to some degree, seen only in two-dimensional form for fundraising campaigns, edgy documentaries and housing benefit rackets. That's certainly not a dig on the great charities and journalists out there, but I'm just saying, it happens. A lot.

The everyday living factors that hundreds of thousands, if not millions of people are living with can be just a conjured-up perception for some. It's through no fault of their own too, it's just they've not personally had a chance to see through those presumptions of a functioning emergency housing system that actually gives people the fighting chance to get back on their feet.

I think a lot of people also fail to consider the true implications of falling out of the system despite the other learnings that can come with it. People such as myself are screaming for employers to take a chance on us, but even for those with some sort of a work history having huge blanks can leave big question marks to employers and for some people good reason.

Again, it's just not all that of a familiar road which people are used to, and despite some of us hoping that the skills we've self-developed might count for something, instead a lot of the time we're just not taken seriously. Maybe one day that will change, and although I know it doesn't happen overnight, perhaps it can for just a small number of people that might be given those chances or taken for what's really inside of them and for what they're really about.

If there's one thing I want to come from this book, it's that I want more employers to acknowledge or at least think about this stigma which exists, but also to be aware and supportive of the playground-like mentality and stitching up that we're constantly facing as one of many target groups.

When you've taken more than enough hits of it in the end you know that some sort of unspoken phenomenon is happening where the disregard for your basic rights of peace are so blatant and widespread that you're stopped in your tracks for standing your ground and too often put into an unwinnable situation of which you want to leave by that point anyway, and so eventually many stop applying for new roles and in the end it becomes a fight to find your faith in people again and reground.

Of course, sadly it's true that among those on the fringes such as those with care leaver and homeless backgrounds that a small number of us for whatever reason will never truly rehabilitate to living and functioning in the so-called normal world. They are at least still having some sort of human experience I guess, but that certainly doesn't account for the many people constantly trying to make something of themselves and coming across all sorts of barriers that really needn't be there.

As for the exterior wear-and-tear of some of us, it has its knock-on consequences. When impressions, perception and prejudice gets in the way of actual connection it's no wonder our newspapers and media channels are full of police incompetence and abuse scandals because often we can judge the very people who are experiencing being stigmatized as psychotic and crazy without really hearing their stories. Perhaps they are somewhat psychotic by some point, but through no fault of their own for those that have craved for a type of connection that isn't always there.

People have their own ways of coping and get used to it but it still doesn't remove the psychological stigma as well as the constant voice from others that tells them that they shouldn't protest any mistreatment from anybody, and that accepting the bare minimum from life is some sort of aspiration future. Perhaps it's easy that way, less drama. Still though, it took me many years to finally click that this was a 'thing' and one I hope others like myself can come forward to express in their stories too.

But despite many of us in general being able to find moments of happiness within the times of hardship, painting a rainbow over it still doesn't make the things that pave those roads right or just. Some can face the stigma so often that they can spend their whole lives bouncing from pillar to post – only to be labelled as the drifter and the drop out as if all completely by choice or all history or experience has simply been erased. On the outside it can all appear as if completely by choice for those with selective sight or an unenquiring tongue.

It's only perhaps now with the recent surge in voices from striking workers and unions, and even since post-edit of online personal development coaches that the issues of exploitation and the lack of respect and decent human treatment is coming to the surface of public awareness.

With no disrespect intended whatsoever to anyone, perhaps finally we have a voice since those like me knew that a lot of people wouldn't care much about the abuse, neglect and exploitation until it had seeped into an obvious state within society.

Not that we ever wished it on anyone either, but perhaps the elements of exploitation and abuse have been allowed to happen in plain sight for so long that it has had more than enough chance to grow. Perhaps now really is the time for a mass awakening though, one that recognises the difference between good and evil, or at the very least – toxic and damaging dynamics.

All this homeless and mental health stigma that I keep banging on about is in some ways linked to the same elements as racism, and could indeed have its subtle far-right elements at times which isn't always immediately obvious. But keep your eyes and ears open long enough and you'll see it about along with its ability to completely infest and corrupt whole environments.

Saying that though, even the unintentional stigma is widespread and across the board, of which until caring characters among us step out of the box to truly connect with such people then they've pretty much not got a voice among anyone. Again though, post-edit of this book I can now see that it is finally growing.

Perhaps the genuine mixture and variety of people in our culture will be respected again and seen as sacred on a much more substantial level than it currently is, where often we base perceived value on a person by the style of their clothes, the bricks and mortar they own or the success that we see them have. We all know there's more to it than that really anyway, but maybe we need start recognising who really needs us to have their backs to bring health, remedy and honesty to a situation, and who are the ones undermining anyone's authority and making them yet another flying monkey in the same old vampire game which too often secretly bites into our culture.

Although both hardship and homelessness can happen to anyone for a variety of reasons, I still find it amazing how many worlds away people can seem to separate themselves from the realities that they catch a glimpse of, often forgetting in some ways I think that these are real people that have real feelings and real-life events.

Perhaps not everyone understands what it's like to walk through life almost completely alone. But perhaps the golden nugget in our lives was that of seeing and appreciating the real value in people coming together to create whatever warmth and light that they could.

It's far too easy though to put everyone all into one box which I suppose we're all guilty of sometimes, yet every one out there considered drifters or homeless each has our own story and unique set of circumstances. During my times as a runaway teen I'd met many different sorts of people from petty criminals to polite people with completely posh accents. As we're all coming to learn over the last decade or so - mental health can be a fragile thing for anyone. Not that I can speak for what happens in everyone's minds, but I've just got the sense that often people haven't thought much more about homeless people as being anything much more than traumatised mental health tragedies.

Perhaps we forget that most people think and feel about family, have dreams they might want to accomplish and most likely don't want to choose to be drop outs living what on the outside can seem a free-spirit and care-free lifestyle.

Let's not forget also, whilst such widespread systemic abuse has been happening right in front of our very eyes, in order for that to happen it's taken those that benefit from it to guide our perception of reality in certain directions. Manipulators and exploiters aren't far away from anybody, and so those used to living the life of clinching onto perceived power have spent generations grooming society into hating on the very people they systematically abuse and outcast.

That in itself brings devastating consequences to a person's mental health, with those that simply don't understand why so many people respond to them the way that they do left completely baffled and bewildered whilst life seems to simply carry on as normal for others.

Perhaps after reading this, despite those that might still fail to grasp where I'm coming from and claim that I'm out for some sort of sympathy or that I'm playing the victim, I'm hoping that more of you will be able to spot this situation when it happens to others that are simply trying to get on with their lives but are trapped within some sort of systemic battle.

Some will of course refute my claims of this phenomenon of a lack of respect, disregard and mistreatment of those not ticking familiar boxes, but there's only so much that you can try to prove to those people before realising that there's no point because some people are so stressed and confused they simply feel that they need that outlet of hate. Essentially, more people just need to be given the chance and seen for their ethics, opinions and beliefs and perhaps thrive most in a team where those making key decisions can see the woods through the trees.

Until then though, many more people that could have gone on to provide real value for a company will continue losing their jobs only to be replaced by yet another number. The Machiavellians at play will not reveal their true thoughts and feelings about such a departure, often acting dumbfounded or surprised about it. For most part everything just carries on as normal for everyone else and nobody really thinks much of it having placed a cushion around their distorted version of events.

Such people muscled out of their jobs by social vampires are quick to be labelled as crazy or not being able to cope with the job once the symptoms of workplace toxicity appear, but I think it would be more substantial and productive to start asking the question - why? There really is a phenomenon of people that condone it, almost as if disregard and abuse towards such people are a default setting. Madness in my eyes, but simply seen as normal reality to many people out there.

Chapter Five – Disregarding and underestimating naturally developed skills.

Some of us can go decades of our lives before realising how little we're often taken seriously, more so sometimes for those which stand out a little more in their own way. Despite not always seeing it ourselves around us there are those that can smell it a mile off and try to take advantage of the fact that you're a person that few take at face value.

Perhaps the biggest reason that those types often eventually go on to see you as a real threat is because for most part they soon learn that despite having gotten away with their games for so long, often simply through instinct we're the first ones to see right through the bullshit.

It's somewhat of a paradox world which I'd quickly learned as a runaway on the streets of London. There were many thousands of people passing me every day that had no real clue that I was a child, but certain people, more predatory ones would still sniff it out immediately.

Some of us get told that we can get taken advantage of sometimes because of our trusting and social nature - which has been a difficult concept for me to process because of those misplaced perceptions about mental strength, intelligence and male pride.

See, even I'm guilty of thinking in such a way though, but it's hard to accept when people tell me that, because for those of us it's happened to - we're not even seeing it as a game worth playing, as it's largely unwinnable anyway in regards to the bigger picture in many environments. We simply don't see that needless chaos, division and toxicity as 'being taken advantage of' as there's no purpose to it all and it causes more fruit to rot than it ever bears.

Eventually though after the situation has repeated so many times it becomes somewhat of a long-term embarrassment that even after expressing such consistent events people can simply presume that you're a pushover. You're not, you just know the difference between those key decision makers that heal a situation between those standing by and enjoying the drama.

Perhaps it wouldn't have such an impact on a person if they weren't looked upon as simply being in some sort of ultra-desperate situation. I think those pushing us into corners that we're constantly fighting out of know all too well of our limited options and opportunities, which is why even seemingly civil people can gradually go on to manipulate, exploit and abuse those from backgrounds like myself because many of them presume we think like them, and that losing our home or our job is the complete end of the world for us when really most of the time we're so uncontrollable that we're happy to say "fuck the money, I'd rather be free and at peace" a lot of the time.

Going deeper into that though, often only those that have witnessed it for themselves will truly understand what it's like to grow into this world in such a way. Sure, there are people that have done some real damaging and selfish things to have themselves put at a safe distance from those within their own families, whilst many more are simply

bafflingly and constantly turned away from the people they thought
had cared about them.

There are very little if any birthday celebrations in these worlds, nor
hospital visits, family photo memories or any of that. Although I'm not
meaning to blow my own trumpet here, I know for sure the long-term
damage that such feelings can take, but at the same time man I feel
like a complete fucking warrior for saying it despite feeling somewhat a
little worn-out and damaged these days.

But without concentrating too much on the somewhat normal
elements of life that we don't have, one of the main purposes of this
book is to highlight the many different perspectives and lived
experiences that I believe need to be acknowledged, valued and
embraced more by today's society generally.

Whilst the general public catches on to trending exploitation,
corruption and abuse scandals perhaps people had just never listened
to some of us within society that were shouting it out right to their
faces. "Meh, psychotic and crazy" many of them said.

Those that have had turbulent lives similar to my own are often
severally underestimated for their ability to spot when damaging
situations are unfolding. Those characters out there that you'll find
trying to manipulate a home, a group, an organisation or the
workplace will no doubt certainly try to paint those like myself in a bad
light to others.

Another purpose of writing this book is in the hope that less people
fall for those slurs and daggers because too often I see what can feel
like a spell that is cast completely bewitch the people around them,
and it becomes difficult to tell the difference between who is genuinely
blinded by the situation and who are those silently revelling in the
sadism.

The thing about being underestimated or being deemed as having low standards is that folk will often reveal all sorts to you. After all, who's gonna take *you* seriously?

I've found myself in a fair few different environments I'll tell you that, and sometimes it doesn't matter who you are really, you just hear the stores. I'll get more into the concept of stalking later on, but in this book I want to also highlight how despite the convictions we see on newspaper headlines how many people are dismissed upon any worries about it when these are things that go on every day in the criminal world.

Just like homeless we see safeguarding systems and presume that they work, but what about the people that actually seek help either through mental health services or even the police? I'm sure many others as well as myself have been through the experience of it being batted-off, as if it doesn't even happen. Yet again – "Hello? Hellooo? Anybody out there?"

Some of the things I'd see and hear as a kid in the east end were far enough from some peoples reality that for many it was something they'd only ever seen in films, yet if some of these professionals had found themselves in such vulnerable positions before or had grown up witnessing what actually happens on the criminal grapevine then perhaps their understanding of life and empathy for people going through such events would have been much more different.

With all of the talk of policing and incompetence scandals, for anything to be truly acknowledged it's important we admit the lack of respect and the mistreatment that many decent and well-meaning people have faced.

Often, it's the people that either have very little or everything to lose that are going out of their way to protect others from harm when life has brought them to such a situation, whilst too often those that are making a living from claiming to do so are bafflingly turning their heads and brushing it all under the carpet. After numerous times you accept that they're ushering you away with their hand and that you're just not deemed worthy enough in their eyes to be taken seriously.

However, with the current state of trust from the general public towards the police - those that have wondered if it was simply their experience can find some sort of relief in knowing that it's a widespread problem that needs a total shift in perspective, and a better learning of human behaviours as well as a realising that people on the streets have seen a lot of stuff.

As for child abuse and grooming, I guess many of us have seen what it's like to be vulnerable prey, but unlike those that couldn't stand up for themselves for whatever reason, often those like me would do their best at fighting back however they could. But I guess such people are also the ones to explain what it's like to be stunned and have delayed reactions too, which are some of the processes often overlooked which I'll go further into later on in this book.

It's taken me a while to understand how my own personal damage and experiences have numbed me enough to be able to talk about the darkest topics of abuse towards children so effortlessly. I remember the time before I truly understood it, in which a friend of mine had seemed almost obsessed. But whenever they'd brought it up I'd always found the conversations off-putting. But then when something really hits and shocks you, and you know that things need to change, it's all too easy to forget how dark a subject it really is, especially to those still learning about those worlds.

For some people it triggers deep trauma, for others it unleashes too much family turmoil and disruption to their peace. But I also believe that for those that have been fortunate enough to not experience it - witnessing any expression of such stories can simply seem too harrowing and alien as if a rare sort of event that only happens in some place over in another foreign land.

I think a lot of people get perceived as unstable once the symptoms of frustration, rage, hopelessness and even psychosis can also be misunderstood by those that haven't yet experienced what it's like to see the entire world turning its back on various things that it proudly claims to be against.

Even if they've had no real education on grooming or abusers - many street folk and drifters have enough experience of being the target that even on levels that they don't always understand they'll still pick up on it. I do believe that however misunderstood many such as myself are - you may indeed just find yourself a few masters of the subject among us.

But until the world truly acknowledges this stigma enough to start reforming it, and brings those like myself into a valued place into their environments, systems and realities – then there's very little that we can make of that knowledge that lays within. First off, you need people to listen, and even when it seems that they respect you you'll will never know if they truly do until you've heard their reaction when you most needed them.

For some us, the journey becomes trying to find those that see it as a shame rather than just 'how it is' to see that environments, organisations and companies are losing out on some genuinely good and useful people through not acknowledging this sort of systemic abuse.

Again, the same old scapegoating comes into play, and when a person deemed as exploitable actually stands their ground then you'll soon discover how the elitist-style viciousness shows how the claim for equal treatment is seen as insulting to some people. The more that we stand our ground against workplace psychopathy the more that we're apparently the issue, and then it's us that's the disruptor.

Being taken by decision makers as unstable, anxious or even psychotic whilst in the midst of cryptically engineered situations is even more awkward if you're the new person in whatever environment that you're in. For a newcomer to a situation the unsurety of trust and respect, along with the sense of isolation can cause detrimental mental health effects upon noticing that others find themselves quickly sucked into the heightening and somewhat bonding feeling of being closer to the group whilst another is being scapegoated.

We've seen it enough times that by some point we're often the first to recognise it happening to others, and can easily find ourselves siding with and even standing up for the scapegoat - which despite providing some sense of relief and support for those that need it can in unhealthy environments cause one's personal situation to be just that little more uncomfortable again. But with not being here to get sucked into any playground popularity contests we find our own strength and relief through a sense of pride, however isolated and uncomfortable certain groups are making us feel again.

Accepting that some people haven't been fully programmed to be simply another cog in a too-often dysfunctional system, is in itself often undervalued. Sometimes an unorthodox path of learning the world can teach things that some people didn't even know had existed. People can overlook that many of these folk were creating hustles to survive along the way, or had no choice from day one but to develop certain social skills to connect with the world around them.

For some, a subconscious knowing of the pain that something can cause is enough to naturally, and without too much thought, want to prevent further needless chaos and harm happening to others. Not that many of those particular stories ever reach our stratosphere.

Despite trying my best to live some sort of honest life these days, there were certain skills and grifts that I'd learned as a teenager growing up that could have served me well materially in adult life. Not that they were ethical, and I went on to try my best to rebel against those unthought-out and desperate temptations. I'd learned back then that more often than not people preferred being marketed to by having their psychology and emotions messed with, and been weaved a well-crafted story rather than interact with the most truthful and genuine of mindsets out there.

Whilst the general public were handing out twenty-pound notes to those with such grifts, it wasn't uncommon for me to constantly observe those that were simply struggling going weeks without anyone reaching out to them. The best beggars and grifters were those that either dressed purposefully as really destitute, or purposefully really smart, with those in-between not having enough of a aesthetical shock value in many people's eyes to even be noticed.

Being so young had helped me when it came to people leaving me food completely off their own back. It hadn't taken me long though to learn that in that world you don't really get anywhere if you don't find a way of standing out. If anything taught me that, it was the time at thirteen years old when I went many days without a single thing, and had been so exhausted that I'd been crying out to thousands of people among the passing public for help, but nothing.

On that particular day, eventually I stole a sandwich from a shop and bolted out of the door, but that's not my point here.

I knew quickly that I had learn a gimmick, and unlike some of the addicts on the streets that I knew that were purposefully getting soaking wet and putting on pitiful faces as part of the grift, I'd decided to follow the advice an old street drinker had taught me in

Whitechapel when I was twelve, which was to try and make people laugh.

Whilst living rough on Piccadilly as a young teen, upon asking the passing public for spare change and sometimes hearing in return "Sorry mate" I'd quickly reply back with "Credit card?" I'd soon worn it out though and mixed things up a little bit, but more often than not it had resulted in unexpected laughter which would often land me a pound or two.

For some of us, the ability to connect as well as make sure that no-one is left out of the fold can be a natural given. It's too often overlooked that many people out there simply don't have that sort of confidence, in which some of those witnessing it can even find it overwhelming and off-putting. That confidence can easily be smashed to pieces later on in life however when it simply isn't recognised or valued, especially in a world where so many people tell you to keep your head down and try to fit in.

However, when such a person finds a team or a company that can appreciate and embrace those traits then good things can happen as long as everyone's not being hoodwinked by jealous manipulators that will do all that they can to understate a person's skills or abilities once they see others have started to see value in them.

Of course, there are also many traumas and perceived negatives which those choosing to bring those in from backgrounds like myself might wish to consider.

The most extreme cases aside, the fact that some of us are claiming to experience this deeply-woven stigma on a frequent basis can lead to many negative and detrimental mental health effects as well as impacting on their social life.

It's all too easy to lose confidence that anyone will take you seriously or see any value in what you do in the end, and a bright spark from a once-young spirit can easily diminish over time. Of course, this is the abusers end goal even to a systemic level, and I think it's something that needs to be considered when reflecting on a person journey through life.

If you're a project leader, an employer or any type of manager of a team, then letting someone know that you can see the hidden elements of scapegoating at play can make all of the difference when keeping valuable team members and uprooting unhealthy work dynamics.

Sure, there are places in the world for competitiveness, but too often the ethos is skewed and merely becomes a self-defeating and toxic trait of a setting or organisation. Whilst everyone there solidifies to each other that they are a team that treats people well, in such cases they are merely deceiving themselves.

Perhaps in today's world also our perception of workplace bullying can also be skewed. The word in itself can give false impressions that a person is simply unable to stand their ground - when actually when it comes to systemic problems within society this is actually far from the case.

Whilst those outspoken and often genuine are sometimes seen as psychotic or aggressive, in my own experience it is often the masters of manipulation that cause toxicity in the workplace whilst giving the appearance that they are keeping their heads down or being professional.

For many, no matter what they do, if people are automatically and subconsciously siding with that perception then those going through it know deep down that they're fighting a losing battle in which the detrimental effects of just trying to hang in there become all too obvious.

Chapter Six– Sometimes it's almost everything

Sometimes the world in which I think I'm living or at least trying to create is often at a paradox with the one that I'm actually doing my best to function in, and that in itself doesn't often lead to the most pleasurable of results. If people are going to truly understand homelessness then perhaps it's important to take on board that many out there on the fringes have spent their whole lives being pulled and pushed from pillar to post, or just simply rejected and denied any sense of a normal relationship even by those seemingly closest to them.

It's something that not everyone can truly comprehend regarding its effects on both day-to-day living and long-term well-being. Such a life circumstance can make or break a person, but still it can take many years to begin to understand why some people don't appear to care about the same things that you do.

Despite naturally assuming that people would get behind our ventures of limiting harm and abuse, instead some of us get deemed simply as unique characters and misfits. I guess in there somewhere is a lesson for all campaigners to be patient with their endeavours because the unexpected reality-flip of seeing the world not really caring about it's bigger picture can be a big hit for anyone to handle, especially when life has shaped you to naturally react to the most devastating of its problems in such a way.

For many, the sense of loneliness can be so real that they wonder how long it would take for anybody to even notice that we were missing. I think those that have always been a part of a strong family unit more often than not fail to understand what it's like for those that seek other ways to compensate for that.

Walking the road of becoming the somewhat regular 'adoptee' of other people's friends and family groups can provide moments of connection, yet can also bring mental confusion for those still feeling 'on the outside looking in'. For some of us it can provide awkward feelings of imposter syndrome and simply not wanting to be a burden on other people's reality even when that really isn't the case.

For as many people there are that are out there crashing on friend's sofas, there are possibly just as many keeping many of their most destitute of situations to themselves because of the embarrassment of people continuing to seeing the struggle.

It's been tough to accept over time that whilst seeing a lot of my peers progressing in their work lives, endeavors and gaining much more immediate support and momentum for their projects - for me, despite a small number of people getting behind me I've mostly been the hundred-to-one outsider in a lot of the things that I do even when it's not a competition.

That had become more than evident after writing *Poems From a Runaway* where the constant social media posts, press-release blasts to thousands of organisations and even telling people that I'd known had often been me just completely shooting in the dark which a lot of the time had brought minimal results. I ploughed on though, and had even started to look at one of my favourite boxers for inspiration, Dillian Whyte.

For those unfamiliar to boxing, he's a rugged but dedicated athlete that had somewhat been unfairly denied his chances to fight in championship bouts with having to wait much longer than others despite being the mandatory contender for years. Coming from Brixton and being a father at thirteen years old, he himself seems to have had to fight relentlessly for his fair shout at things, and so often I'd use that feeling of relentless underdog spirit to help keep me going.

It worked for a short while too, but for a much of it until now I've struggled to even give my creations away, in which I've started to develop my own quotes over time about how even if I was selling the most delightful of food or a load of gold bars for fifty pence each, still nobody want them from me. A deep feeling that I pray I can one day find a way of resolving, find my faith again and be at connection with the energies if that's even what it is.

But those are the least damaging of people's wounds when it comes to almost every family relationship being like that. For years I've been aching for friends and family to tell me why I'm so off their radar. Surely there's a reason? Surely it's me?

We ourselves can even disregard the stigma whilst wondering if this is some sort of unrecognized personality issue within us, but the frustration that nobody at all will explain why they repeatedly turn their backs on you can be a tough one to comprehend, especially when you know that you're the type of person that can take it on board without having a hissy fit.

Despite contemplating if I'm merely solidifying some sort of 'victim' complex, in many ways even writing this book has only made me realise that my experience is in fact very real, yet it can be even more damaging when so many people try to convince you that it's not.

For many, it takes its mental toll and even if things are seeming to be working out ok then you're still half-expecting the next life event to pop up and send you straight back to square one again, if depression hasn't done that already by some point.

Just like others that have had to shout loud for a better standard of inclusion in society by default we're up against it.

It's one reason why I think that we have a completely engineered criminal class. There are all sorts of people with skills, passions and talents that legitimately want to be a contributing member of society, but through the constant systemic abuse many that didn't have the fortune of learning to play a guitar like me and earn enough for a sandwich to get by during their most desperate of times were often left with nothing more than the dangerous concoction of malnutrition, stress and emotional turmoil.

Sometimes I wonder if learning to play the guitar was the difference in me becoming a person that society tolerates - to becoming a person that society hates and mobs. Maybe I would have made more mistakes out of pure desperation, only to be labelled as a thug, a thief or simply a criminal.

The cookie-cut standard appearance of a roadmap to life seems all-too clear-cut to those that say if only everyone worked hard enough at something then they'd get there. But perhaps until we've acknowledged such societal issues then crime will always be rampant.

The huge contradiction in today's reality though is that whilst those from backgrounds like myself that end up involved in crime are seen somewhat as vagrants, both under the surface and out there on show in worlds such as TikTok and the like, instantly the ethos is flipped and all of a sudden it's fashionable.

I'm certainly not advocating for criminality, but merely trying to explain that when you strip away the veils of respectability and civil behaviour in what for a while had seemed a stable society, if the show suddenly ends and the music stops - only then in such true tests will you really see who is who and understand how desperate anybody can get.

It's not a popular opinion that everybody wants to accept, that many of those in prison are there because of an ever-so-fragile system that in many areas leaves hundreds or thousands of people all applying for the same jobs, in which among those people some simply don't stand much of a chance.

The same old 'I'm alright Jack' quotes get bantered around regardless, in which common understanding and possibly empathy is tossed aside in the claim that those people should be able to function psychically, mentally and emotionally on the minimum of state benefits and support networks. Perhaps they can eventually if they keep the vision, but let's be under no illusion here that there are a lot of people really struggling through this.

Those that dare treat themselves to a pack of cigarettes or a Netflix subscription for their children despite not remembering the last time that they ever had a family holiday are merely scapegoated in the media by the same old vicious voice that comes usually from entities that seek to get you hating the products of a problem, instead of the actually problem itself.

Don't listen to me though, just lock them all up and throw away the key. No, don't. You know what I'm saying!

As for my housing situations over the years, I'd often witnessed a huge disconnection of understanding between those that have had to use the emergency housing system, and those that haven't.

I'll tap into this a little more later, but the perception that someone can just go to the council and get the help that they need is far from the chaotic and draining reality that many experience of basic failings, commercial exploitation and factory-farm style housing benefit rackets that are all too common. What starts as an issue of someone needing a place to stay to get back on their feet can quickly and easily become a person battling all sorts of domestic problems.

Time and energy that could be spent on making some sort of genuine progression in life can easily be sucked away by the more immediate needs of those that have had to settle with the only options that they could find. Hats off to those that managed to climb their way out of such worlds whilst living in shared houses with sub-standard conditions, no sense of security and constant intense situations.

Do those that haven't ever witnessed needing such help with emergency accommodation even understand the sorts of environments our homeless people are often left no choice but to live in?

Imagine the smell of heroin wafting from bedroom doors and the air of institutionalization and you wouldn't be far off many settings that are out there supposedly to help people. "Well, I got on a housing list and it was easy for me" some people condescendingly say, but if for whatever reason someone has to move areas they can find themselves immediately back to square one on any housing waiting lists, if even accepted to be on them at all.

It's clear that there needs to be a radical reform in how emergency housing and homelessness is approached. The current 'one size fits all' template that we currently have merely diminishes the chances for people to live as contributing members of society, instead giving them more obstacles and barriers that had ever been a part of their world in the first place.

For younger adults especially, the system can set them up to fail when reality for others in their age groups is going to college or becoming a valuable trainee of a work team, whilst for others simply trying to find their place in the world one is of their first puzzles.

Then comes working out how to find the motivation to juggle being holding down a new job whilst also living in a shithole.

For those living in ran-down hostels, finding somewhere to live in a quick enough amount of time and being able to save enough money for a deposit can also be difficult for those who have to claim extra housing benefit for the support given, which can in some organisations be questionable.

Before you know it - the police are at the front door every week looking for somebody, and the whiff of heroin can be smelt from peoples rooms. "Just move out then" can seem such a simple answer if only we'd got those numbers in line on the combination lock of life.

For those in this position, put up and shut up is often the status quo. Those that dare express their feelings of injustice or complain about it are told that it's just the way that it is and to quit whining by people that have had the fortune of never experiencing those barriers to a mentally healthy environment.

An environment where one can not only progressive in life to serve economic purposes, but also for reasonable and understandable spiritual growth for those whose lives have already been chaotic and traumatic often to this point.

Chapter Seven – Those few times when stitch up's backfire

When you're young and don't even really realise that the circumstances that have led you to growing up into the world somewhat as a lone solider can in fact make you quite vulnerable despite all of its strengths, realising how at risk such people are of being used like tools for those forever wanting to get ahead in their careers becomes a learning journey in itself . As you will read in the following story, this sort of mentality towards people like myself can have devastating effects, and not only for the scapegoat either.

In my early twenties growing up I clearly remember the huge pile of stop and search forms that I'd collected in my room at one of the London squats that I'd been living in. Whenever I'd notice them again I'd shake my head in disbelief at how many were there.

Nearly always it was when I was busking, and no matter how respectable I'd tried to be I'd often know instantly that I was about to be stopped and searched. It had been tense times in London in those days though since not only the 2001 attack on America's Twin Towers, as well as the London bombings in 2005, but it was also around the start of what would go on to be a phenomenal surge of inner-city knife crime.

In hindsight I've much understanding about the heightened sense of vigilance back then, but almost every time I'd asked why they were stopping and searching me after seeing that I was busking and clearly just a young English lad, the answer was nearly always "because you could be a terrorist."

"Really?" was often my response in what was merely just another moment of being pushed off almost every place that I'd decided to busk. It was not only back then a quite intense time regarding policing in London, but there was now becoming an ever-growing privatization of the city's streets, where even if I wasn't even near buildings I was getting moved on within five minutes by private security firms that simply wouldn't ever bargain one bit for any sort of civil agreement. 'Computer says no, simply move on.'

As for my confused response as to why the police were still going to search me despite not ticking many of the 'terrorist' boxes, they'd often simply reply back with "well what does a terrorist look like?"

In all fairness to the police though, the overall vibe with such experiences did change eventually at some point, and future ones with the police would go on to seem much more positive in the five years or so afterwards in London.

But that wasn't before 2008, when two police officers had not only thrown a brick through a window whilst knowing I was standing right behind it, but had used a sledgehammer to smash down the door and arrest me for possession of cannabis under a fabricated story.

Part of me sometimes wonders how deep the rabbit hole goes with this arrest, but anxieties and paranoia aside, either way it was clear that the officers patrolling the estate that night didn't want me on their patch.

I'd overheard some voices outside of the house before I'd known it was actually the police, and had made my way to the front window to listen easier to a conversation I'd heard about squatters, presumably us. Naively, I'd completely overlooked the fact that a candle that I'd lit in the back of the room would have caused a big silhouette of me standing there behind the big paper sheet that I'd temporarily stuck up during what was now a dark winters evening.

Suddenly the conversation that I was hearing had gone completely quiet which had raised my curiosity somewhat, but just a moment later the window in front of me had then smashed, and immediately I heard something drop onto the floor.

With the unknown object hitting the paper curtain in front of my face and hearing it drop - my first thought was that it was a petrol bomb thrown in by some local squatter-hating vigilante or something. But after scoping the floor to see where whatever was thrown in had landed I'd quickly determined that it wasn't a petrol bomb and soon heard the police sergeant again who was outside and demanding that I open up the door.

Fortunately for me, upon them threatening to smash it down I'd decided to call 999, in which during the call one of the police officers had used a sledgehammer to break down the door and make their way in. After the police sergeant who I'd already had intense encounters with twice before that week had taken my phone after the operator had asked to speak with him - it was then that without really thinking about it that I'd decided to switch on my voice recorder.

Not that I thought that I was being discreet or anything with its bright red light now turned on that should of beamed out to everyone there that it was recording.

It was obvious that the police sergeant was trying to find a joint to arrest me for, in which he paced around the house whilst shouting that I was a lawbreaker. After being told by the other officer with him that I could have simply found a hostel or something and that they didn't want me on their patch, my reading of the section six notice in relation to squatters rights counted for nothing as the two officers decided to drag me out causing me to bash my knee on the doorframe as I was being half-involuntarily forced out.

Accusing me of faking the pain that I was in the police sergeant then pointed to the nearest lamppost which was as far as I still know nothing more than simply a lamppost. "See that there?" he said in his thick Irish accent, "there's a camera in there watching you breaking windows and breaking in."

Instantly I pulled him up on his bullshit and it was only in that moment of delayed thinking that it had clicked in my head that it was them that had thrown towards my head what I later discovered was a stone around the size of an adult's palm, which if it wasn't for the paper curtain stopping its flight it could of caused me a number of injuries. The situation had simply been too intense to even think about what was going on until that point.

After going back into the house and searching it intensely to eventually find what was around a tenners worth of weed, he eventually came back out with it in his hands and arrested me. Upon one of the officers putting the cuffs on me he'd asked me what I was holding in my hands. "A voice recorder" I said to him, in which after asking me what I had it for I simply replied that it was for my music.

Despite that, to me it felt obvious that with the recording displaying it's bright red light that I was recording them, and so whilst now sat in the back of a police van with no windows and in handcuffs I was then imagining the two officers along with the rest of them that had now turned up to be gathered around the voice recorder and trying to work out together how to delete the file.

When I eventually got to the police station, I remember briefly one of the officers telling me that I could either go with their version of events and be let out in a few hours, or instead be in there all weekend. I'd been in such a pissed-off state of mind about the whole saga though that what he'd said to much degree had gone completely over my head at the time.

Upon getting into the station and hearing that the sergeant was falsely telling the custody officer that he'd found cannabis in my pocket and caught me breaking windows, I certainly let my feelings known to them and the other officers around that it wasn't what had happened at all.

I'd blurted out all of the usual frustrations one would have in such a situation, of how much dangerous crime was no doubt happening at the time and here they were fabricating a story and arresting me.

I'd made no silence about the fact that they were keeping me prisoner and misusing the law to essentially kidnap me, but I couldn't help but feel that the other officers around that I'd tried to express it to were simply looking right through me with a blank stare. Not all of them though, which I'd come to later learn despite what I'd initially thought.

I knew it was all just wrong, and so for that - if you think you're going to just misuse your position to treat me like I've done enough to be thrown and locked into a cell then you WILL hear three-hour renditions of Bob Marley, The Beatles and a whole range of nineties covers at full volume, and I can't half belt it out too when I do!

Eventually after much unsuccessful pleading from officers walking down to the cells to stop singing so loud - at some point one officer who'd turned out to be a decent bloke had said that he'd try to get me a ten-minute break outside in the caged area, which had been a sort of outside space-come-entrance leading into the station's custody suite.

Not that he had to do so, but unexpectedly he'd offered me a cigarette too in which I thankfully obliged. "I heard what you were saying early on in there mate, and I believe you" he'd go on to say.

I explained to him what had happened and how what they were saying when they were booking me in had been completely fabricated.

He'd go on to tell me in his own words that he was far from enjoying working there.

Once I finished the cigarette and was taken back to my cell he offered to try and find me a magazine to read from the station canteen or wherever else he could find one.

He'd been gone for a few hours, obviously sidetracked with something or other, which he later explained when I did eventually see him again. "Sorry I've been a while mate, but I've been all over the station and this is all I could find. It's only like a gossip magazine thing, but there's some fit birds and that to look at in there" he'd go on to say.

"Thanks mate" I chuckled back to him having being genuinely appreciative of him counteracting what would of otherwise been quite a sterile and cold experience during my time in those cells. Not that it had been my first time locked up by any means, but it's never exactly a holiday resort is it?

There had in fact been some rather attractive-looking celebrity queens in that magazine like he'd said, and so like any other slightly immature rebellious spirit I'd decided that if this was where I was going to be held captive, then I was going to cut out some of the photos of those women and make the place like some sort of teenagers bedroom by using the last remaining drips of food from my food trays to stick them up with. In the last bit of freedom that I had left for that moment at least, I'd decided that I'd be making the rules.

Soon after that I went full-blown hippy binge once I'd spotted certain words in headlines and articles that I felt would do some good for me up on the wall. Words such as 'Love', 'Light', 'Positivity' 'strength', and 'justice' among many more.

It did do me some good actually, and opposed to the immediate 'fuck you' rage that I'd initially been in, now I was calmer, feeling wiser and stronger, and the weight and tenseness had finally gone from my head and I was now trying to bring in some good energies.

The duty solicitor that came in that night to see me had struck me as being a somewhat intriguing character. Despite his slightly scruffy ginger hair and appearing as if he'd either been up all night or had simply got out of bed and thrown back on his clothes, I remember clearly that he had a bit of a unique 'go' and energy about him.

After introducing himself, he started reading the charges as well as the officers claims about them.

"So, they're saying that you were outside of the property with what appeared to be a cannabis joint that you were smoking. Then when they approached you, you'd ran off into the house before returning back out. They then searched you and found cannabis in your right coat pocket."

"Ay?" I replied.

Sure, I'd been half-expecting some exaggerations in their story to some degree, but not like that.

After telling the solicitor that it wasn't what had happened at all, I'd then remembered the voice recording, and even though I was quite certain that the officers would have made sure to delete it, I still knew that there was a tiny chance that they hadn't of deleted it for some reason.

I hadn't mentioned that specifically to the him, but simply stated that there was a small chance that I could prove it was bullshit.

He got me to write a statement saying that I was inside of the property all day, and that what the officers were saying was a lie and to then stay completely silent for the rest of the interview. He advised me that if I was going to plead not guilty then they'd likely refuse me bail and keep me in there all weekend, but I'd had enough of playing along by that point anyway. Why should I make any of this convenient for them? I thought.

So, I decided to stick it out and not play a part in their bullshit story and charges against me, and certainly wasn't going to play a part in lying for that to happen.

During the interview, the immediate frustration that I wasn't playing along with their game was obvious in the face of the officer that was sat in front of me. I could tell he'd been ultra-annoyed in the way that he'd walked out of the room after the interview with things not going quite to plan. A huge thanks to that solicitor if ever stumbles across this book by any chance.

On Monday morning I was taken straight to court, in which I pleaded not guilty, and with some specific sense of pride in saying so too. Not that I knew at the time if I'd ever be able to prove anything, and even the fact that I'd dialled 999 it was something that I'd completely forgotten about until later on.

Upon being bailed to appear in another magistrates court where there'd be a trial a couple of months afterwards, I was taken back down into the bottom of the courts where I'd be released and given my bag of possessions back.

As well as being given a pack which consisted of a copy of the officer's statements and a cassette copy of the interview recording, there'd been some small chance of hope I'd captured it by that point upon seeing the silver-coloured voice recorder inside of the clear plastic bag of my possessions.

I wouldn't know for sure until I'd got to check it though, and so upon getting released and going upstairs through the public waiting area of the courts, whilst putting the laces back into my trainers I decided to see if by any small chance that the recording had saved and that officers hadn't deleted it.

I'd been surprised to put it mildly to then find that the recording hadn't been deleted, and had completely contradicted everything that the officers had been saying. Not only that, but even though I was trying to listen to it through its tiny built-in speaker whilst sat in a bustling and loud court waiting area, I could just about make out that it was a full and clear recording of everything that had happened since I'd switched it on right up until the point of my arrest.

Still somewhat feeling the strong sense of making sure that I wasn't going to be yet another victim of police injustice and corruption - I shook my head and thought to myself - 'you silly, silly, boys'.

For some reason I'd thought it best to type up the officer's statements as soon as I'd got to a computer, initially because reading the scruffy and rushed handwriting was proving to be difficult. But it soon taught me that it was a great way to analyse the statements in some sort of depth at a controlled pace, and before I knew it I was spotting inconsistencies every few seconds.

It hadn't taken me long to write up an actual in-depth defence case that I could read off in court. Not that I knew how representing myself in court actually worked technically, but the fundamental basics were there at least.

Of course, I likely would have benefitted from a solicitor still though, but being completely trapped out of the system to some degree at the time with no identification, bank account and traceable history for years, I'd been struggling to get a benefits claim going, and so I was merely getting turned away by solicitors every time because I couldn't claim legal aid.

My time leading up to the trial had been a somewhat intense one for me personally, but that could have easily been my fault of not handling it very well. Whilst telling some of the people in my life about the arrest and the recording, one of the people I knew had been one of the only people to suggest that maybe I chose to forgive the officers, and that the power I'd had in my hands could end their careers and ruin their lives, adding that perhaps it would be a bit harsh of me to allow them to be prosecuted.

Whilst everybody else had been congratulating me and hoping that it had prevented others from being stitched up by the officers, I'd grew some suspicions about one of my friends who might well have just been seeing the situation from a different perspective. But at the time it meant that I was being extra cautious about where my recording was, and had ensured that I'd made extra copies which I'd kept somewhere safe elsewhere.

On the day of court, I wasn't sure if they were going to accept my recording as any sort of defence or not. Surely there were legal routes that I had to take to submit those sorts of things I'd thought, but not that I had any real clue what I was doing.

Nevertheless, I'd turned up dressed smartly and had also brought with me my cheap busking amplifier so that I could play the recording to the court.

Still on some sort of strong sense of justice trip, I'd actually been meditating around the corner on some grass before going in to the court. Meditating wasn't something I even did much apart from finding my zen through singing and playing music. But there I was, praying to God and the energies for backup to not have to sit and follow through with a load of lies about what had actually happened on the night of my arrest.

I'd half-expected the court security to take my voice recorder and amplifier upon entry anyway, but even more so after seeing the 'no recording equipment' stickers on the main doors of the court.

I'd then explained to the security guard that I might need to come back for it all to show the courts, in which he then gave me a numbered raffle ticket to hand back to him later on.

As I walked into the waiting area outside of the courtroom that I was soon due to go into, there sat on a row of seats within a corridor was the police sergeant and the other officer that had arrested me. I'd got cocky perhaps, but something in me wanted to let them know for sure that I wasn't going to be intimidated by them, and so I sat immediately opposite them both, looked them both deep into their eyes as if to tell them they hadn't got a clue what was coming.

The sergeant laughed at me smugly, probably thinking how much of a fool I was to think that I was confident to win in court. "You're not still pleading not-guilty are you?" he said whilst laughing condescendingly.

"Yeah" I replied, whilst giving them a look of confidence that beamed out 'bring it on then'.

The police sergeant simply carried on laughing, whilst his colleague, well, I'd spotted a look deep in his eyes in that moment. Perhaps he was sensible enough to pick up on when someone was genuinely confident, but the micro-second of worry as to if I was really bluffing or not had been obvious for a short moment there.

Still though, there never really was any actual bitter hate towards them really from my end, I just wanted to prove myself as not-guilty in court and not have to play into their fabricated version of events.

Upon getting calling in by the court usher I then entered the courtroom at the same time the sergeant had, whilst his colleague waited outside to be called in to give his evidence afterwards.

As soon as I arrived into the court I spoke directly to the three magistrates that were across the room and had explained to them that even though I didn't really know what I was doing having never represented myself before in court, that I did have a defence case that I needed to speak about, and had asked for their patience and guidance in enabling me to do.

I'd been kindly explained to by one of the magistrates that the officers would first give their evidence, in which I'd then get a chance to cross-examine them by asking them some questions if I'd wanted to, which having not been to court for many years I'd not really thought about in advance.

Eventually it had become obvious to the magistrates that the stories didn't quite add up anyway, in which they themselves probed the officers further to check for holes in their stories and were soon spotting them.

But for all of the cockiness still beaming from the police sergeant that he was in control of the situation - things were certainly about to take a somewhat sharp turn once he'd left the courtroom, in which his colleague then came in to give his version of fabricated events about me apparently standing outside of the premises that night before being chased in.

Having explained my side of the story and that I'd dialled 999, as well as switching on my voice recorder, and that the police had broken in - the woman appearing in the leading role for the Crown Prosecution Service had intervened and asked if I had the recording with me, in which after explaining that it was downstairs the court usher had then gone to collect it.

The Crown Prosecution asked everyone else to leave the room so that she could hear the evidence alone. With my cheap amplifier and music leads not performing like they should have immediately, I stayed though to help play it through the amplifier.

Upon hearing it, she apologized to me immediately and stated that she wouldn't have taken on the case if she'd have known about the recording.

Upon the three magistrates returning, she then explained to them that she wanted to drop the case. They'd heard more than enough by that point though to feel concerned.

There'd been moments during the officers' testimonies where I'd caught the look in one or two of the magistrate's eyes, where it had been more than obvious that we could all see the holes in their story. They then explained to the woman from CPS that they were refusing to simply drop the case because they wanted to listen to the recording for themselves.

After what seemed almost an hour of them being away from the courtroom, they all returned to tell me that all of the charges against me were now dropped, and that they were apologizing that this had happened to me, stating that it wasn't one rule for the police and one for everyone else.

They said that I was free to go but would appreciate it if I stuck around as all three of them had made official complaints to the police who were now on their way to come and talk to me.

Eventually after a bit of waiting around and coming to learn that journalists that were already in the courtroom digging for local stories had also now picked up on what was going on, I spoke with a pleasant woman from CID who over the coming few years would be the main investigator alongside the Independent Police Complaints Commission, in what was now a charge against the officers for perverting the course of justice.

It would take around two years or so, but eventually dates had been set for two unintentionally postponed trials before finally going ahead at Southwark Crown Court where I'd go on to give evidence.

It had been a somewhat confusing time by that point, with a lot of my initial rage around the situation somewhat fizzling away. But still, all of this was out of my hands in many ways by that point and they'd brought it on themselves I suppose, like many had told me.

I'd be lying if I said that I wasn't pleased to see that the officers were getting a taste of their own medicine to some degree after having a brick nearly hit my head, but at the same time there was also a slight sympathy of how hard their own abuse of power was now hitting back at them.

The police sergeant in particular looked a bit a wreck with his arrogant demeanour having now completely changed, and I couldn't help but wonder if he'd hit the bottle. Not that I had any feelings of pride about that or anything, but I just remember feeling that his energy had now reminded me of a kid being in trouble at school more than anything. Not to try and be insulting or anything, just that the energy had shifted so to speak.

Despite being told by the judge in court not to speak with any journalists on the way out, having only personally seen one

photographer outside of the courts once anyway, I'd presumed that
there hadn't really been much media interest.

Unknown to me at the time, because I simply wasn't searching for it,
what had started out as a case in London being covered not only by a
local news outlet and also for some reason the Yorkshire post, it had
also been covered by the BBC and briefly by ITV among others.

Years later when I'd found some of those particular articles I'd come
to learn that despite not even being aware of it myself, that the
magistrates from the initial hearing along with the investigating officers
that were prosecuting the sergeant and his colleague as well as the
IPCC - had been more than aware of the stigma and disregard that
such people like myself have lived with.

I'd come to learn of how the prosecution would express that I was
simply somebody that the officers thought didn't matter and wouldn't
be believed, and in all honesty it's taken me years to fully understand
exactly what they'd meant, only due to a personal revelation of how
there really is an unspoken status quo of abuse, disregard and
exploitation affecting whole parts of our own society.

Deep down though, similarly to how my street life had manifested
itself, I was one of the lucky ones having not being shot, raped or
beaten to death. Still though, the age-old quote that someone else
always has it worse only serves as a temporary painkiller and does very
little to combat the infection.

The Metropolitan Police had certainly taken it seriously anyway with
the cost of the case being in the millions of pounds. I'd also come to
learn of other happenings, events relating to the officer's too, which
had revealed itself to me from those that were trying their best to
change the system and ethics of policing from within.

After giving my evidence at the trial, I left and awaited the call back from the Detective Sergeant who'd put together the case alongside the IPCC.

She'd been extremely apologetic when she called later that day, explaining that because the evidence was audio and not visual that the judge had ordered the jury to dismiss the evidence.

She'd begged me to hang in there though, stating that even though the officers had been found not guilty on a technicality that the police were now taking them to an internal misconduct hearing in which I wouldn't have to wait too long for. The detective sergeant explained that if I could give evidence just once more at the hearing then it would all soon be over.

It'd be fair to say that by that point I was starting to feel a little drained by it all and just wanted to close the book on it. Despite not feeling too proud in saying so, there were times I almost did give up and thought 'screw it', just wanting the whole scenario to be an old chapter of my life by that point and move on so to speak. Equally though, I'd enjoyed the feeling of the sense that I was doing the right thing, but also the recommendation by the detective sergeant to put in a compensation claim was certainly something which had helped me to keep going at some point.

After giving my evidence at the misconduct hearing a few months later which was a new experience in itself, the police officers that had framed me were immediately dismissed from the force later on that day.

I was glad for it all to be finally over, in which the detective sergeant thanked me for sticking it out until the end when she'd called me to let me know the result of hearing. A few months afterwards I was offered a civil payout from the Met Police of which after being advised to push for more by my solicitor, after a further settlement offer from the police, I then thankfully obliged.

With still struggling to get ID and references, I didn't have a bank account at the time, so I was keeping my money in a credit union account down in Brighton. Sure, perhaps if I'd have had a little more guidance or a sense of stability then I'd have made much better decisions with it. Still though, it was my first lesson in learning about handling such amounts of money that I'd never seen before or since.

I'd found it surprising how hard it was to still find a place with limited references and no guarantor even though I'd had the money to put at least half a years worth of rent down in advance. I got there in the end though after moving into a house with some music students, but still I can't help remembering shaking my head at feeling like I was still facing so many barriers in front of the seemingly simple things in life.

Throughout the process of the whole case it had certainly been an interesting time in regards to my shifting opinions of the police. Despite still witnessing some intense and even slightly strange encounters involving the police whilst I'd been living and protesting with some of the anti-war activists in Brighton, some police officers had surprised me by bringing up the case that I was in involved with and congratulating me and wishing me luck.

I actually hadn't known at the time that the whole case was being discussed not only on forums mainly consisting of cannabis smokers that had picked up on the news, but also on police forums from all over the UK and the world.

As expected, there were of course some dividing opinions on the police websites, but largely there'd been a general tone of admitting that the officers should have stuck to doing things by the book, and it seemed largely that there'd been little sympathy for them.

I remember being at one demonstration whilst down in Brighton before I'd gone to the trial at Southwark, where one police officer had stuck out his hand to shake mine, congratulated me on the case and asked me how I was getting on.

Despite at the time being completely paranoid that the people I'd been among at the demonstration now thought that I could have been in with the police or an informant, deep down it had been a pleasant change of spirit from what I'd known previously of my encounters with the police whilst up in London, and I was always too much of a free-spirit anyway to worry about it too much to be honest.

Plus, perhaps it took me a while to truly realise the frustrations of the police officers out there that are genuinely good and decent people. They're the ones that will see the factors that can cause the public to have their reasons for holding a painful hate towards the police as an institution, and only now in 2023 have I heard spoken publicly from within the police force words with such true-sounding depth of how needlessly and tragically they've been letting a lot of people down.

From failing to intervene when officers are displaying seriously unprofessional and abusive standards to completely disregarding and stonewalling abuse victims and whistleblowers are just some of the many things in the public's mind these days.

Whilst recently watching a press conference held by current Met Police Commissioner Mark Rowley, it had been the first time that I'd ever heard publicly from the police such an admittance that they're in a code red situation, and were admitting that they need to reach out to the public to share their experiences and stories to help fix what has become an absolutely unprecedented systemic failing to acknowledge not only professional standards, but in some cases the more basic elements of human respect, treatment and a true sense of value for life.

However, relating to other events that I'll explain further into this book not everyone is a lucky as I was in such a situation. Not only because they wouldn't have had a voice recorder or a phone to dial 999 - but part of me sometimes wonders what would have actually been the outcome of my initial hearing if one of the magistrates there hadn't have been of black ethnicity, which had likely made him more familiar with the patterns and red flags of when police are abusing their powers whilst stigmatising certain people.

What if I hadn't of had such luck though, perhaps by been in a completely different area in the country, and not had anyone there with that same passionate desire to make a stand to say that those things shouldn't be happening to people.

That's certainly not to understate the phenomenal talent that oozes through all different parts of life in this country, but I don't feel that we're being honest with ourselves if we fail to admit that despite aesthetics - that some work cultures haven't moved that far from the 1980's, perhaps we're just more snidey with it these days and failing to admit it.

Either way, it goes to show that even prosecutors, complaints commissions and many police are more than well aware of the amount of systemic disregard for some sections of society there is. They're the ones that see most the phenomenal amounts of abuse that is completely mis-labelled as normal behaviour by people that have convinced themselves that they're more respectable and entitled to decent standards of treatment than others.

It's a struggle that is happening across the board. An attempt of reshaping human consciousness and emotional intelligence to some degree, which is always a little hard in what has become a world overran by those that want to bleed you and keep your mind on a hamster wheel of constant stress, where there often isn't even much time to contemplate how you're really feeling, let alone how somebody else is.

If I can have confidence in one thing about this book and about the things that I'm saying in it, it's that similarly to when I'd started the Neuroliberation campaign - and felt that nobody had been really taking my concerns about the gambling industry seriously. Despite the lack of general support at the time, interestingly, journalists and television producers were often the ones giving me the chance to voice my statements regarding it all.

Nowadays everybody's talking about dopamine too like I was back then, but I always knew with my life the way it often panned out that I'd accepted my role as simply a seed planter, an ideas man to inspire someone else. Big ideas too perhaps, and often requiring far more resources and investment than I could ever provide. But if it made even one person with the ability to do so to decide to make a positive impact in the name of a healthier and safer society then in my eyes it would of all been worth it.

So for those thinking about sharing their stories but worry that they'll simply appear dramatic or crazy even though they know they're not, I truly hope that this book inspires them to share them with the world, because no matter how many people bafflingly turn their heads away and stand with their back to you - there's always someone out there that understands exactly what you're going through .

For all of the people that tell you through words or lack of them that your genuine deepest concerns aren't worthy of acknowledgement, perhaps it's time to rebel and embrace the attitude of 'ain't nobody got time for that'. I do believe this is simply the merging future that some still haven't had the fortune of learning and processing themselves into it yet, a reconnection with our more humane and spiritual side. For those feeling a little lost and confused with it all at the moment, hang tight just a little longer.

Chapter Eight – Losing Faith

Pre-warning, this chapter covers the subjects of child abuse and surrounding subjects

Having lived among a group of anti-war activists in one of the squats in Brighton that I was in around the time of the big court case, on one particular evening the front door had been smashed in by the local police just the day before some of them had planned a demonstration in the city centre.

Completely smashing to pieces what had been quite a beautiful and large front door whilst entering the house under the false pretence of searching for a nearby suspicious character - the police had kept us inside of the building throughout the whole night until they'd finally taken everybody's names.

Me and the other housemates thought that it would be the end of it but the police had manned the house hallway all night and waited for someone from the power company to arrive in the morning and rip out the electric wires from the main box before then simply leaving us with a house with no electricity box.

Unknown to me at the time, what I'd first thought were simply new faces and acquaintances of some of my newfound friends that I'd been living with, they'd actually been offered to stay there during the protests on some online forum or other.

Upon going to the demonstration in town for a bit that day, with the sheer numbers that were there it wasn't any surprise really that the police or public order intelligence unit were keeping tabs on it all and trying to influence things by keeping us up all night in the house.

I'd seen the echoes of political policing and undercover intelligence before during my times in Brighton after discovering an anarchist bookshop with a café and bar, which had consisted of many of the area's proudly left-wing movers and shakers. I'd met some great people among various motley crews of misfits that would find themselves there, but too often because of the tough political battles and direct action that some were putting themselves to it had also attracted the attention of the far right, undercover police, informers and agent provocateurs.

It had made it feel somewhat off-putting at times, causing certain cliques that I could see had failed to welcome in some of the people with a burning desire to make change simply because of the suspicions and paranoias that had been around due to the well-founded suspicion of infiltration.

Who's to say that the authorities or the far right didn't have a man on the inside anyway? But even though I'd been invited to one or two meetings about anti-war demonstrations happening in town - I'd never truly felt comfortable at some of those behind-closed-doors meetings being somewhat of an unintentional nomad who nobody really knew very well, and there was always the looming anxiety of if they thought I'd been a plant or something.

But despite all of those subtones and themes in my mind at the time regarding the police, and even though there were a couple of other odd moments that I remember in Brighton relating to them, generally the whole court case and prosecution against the officers that had set me up in London had actually largely restored my faith in the police for a while.

Unfortunately, all of that was about to be completely undone a few years later when I moved areas and had found myself on a completely new journey. It was a journey where for all my times living on the streets as a teenager, or in my turbulent life as an adult, I never knew how little I really knew about one subject in particular. I'm talking about grooming and abuse towards children.

Like a lot of people, I thought I knew all there was to know about it. Creepy old men outside parks, strangers enticing schoolkids into their vehicles and the stereotypical dodgy uncle so often used in dark British humour.

Instead though, it would soon reveal to me that despite my street past perhaps making me a little more hyper-sensitive than some in regards to being able to pick up on the more subtle sins of grooming, being able to actually fully know and translate what I was sensing at times became a whole new journey in itself.

And I know no matter what anyone thinks, it's perfectly alright to accept that we don't always see the signs, and it's not always through any fault of our own too. Most people would want to presume that they're completely on the ball, all wise and knowing and can never be fooled, and admitting that a person might not have always been able to spot when such risk in a situation arises can be an awfully tough thing for anyone to accept.

Despite some of us finding ourselves on this journey in what can only be described as the most synchronistic way possible, I'll bypass some of the more spiritual moments and synchronicities that led me there and try to keep my writings on this topic as factual, simple and clear as I can.

For all of our banding together on social media to comment on headline cases such as Jeffrey Epstein, Jimmy Saville and whoever is next in line to be exposed as operating right under our noses, one of the hardest fights for child abuse campaigners still to this day is getting people to use at least some of that energy into showing that concern within their own environments and communities.

Whether it's people willingly letting the subject go right over their heads, or if it's simply too much for them to fathom, those others that dare speak out on such issues know all too well how hard it really is to get people to listen, let alone act.

The paradox of those that know too little about it - and those that know too much - can often leave a gaping void for anyone trying to expose such abuse. Whilst watching internet commentators on high-profile media cases now becoming self-proclaimed child abuse activists, others among us are all too familiar with knowing that when people really need support to tackle such issues - for some of us nobody is there at all despite the message being broadcast loud and clear.

It's something that I think the world is in a process of acknowledging and admitting, that something about our lives or our consciousness is preventing us naturally reaching out to protect others in the world around us, despite all of our claims that it's what we do.

My own personal journey into this world revealed a lot to me about how it all happens under the radar, yet so many of the signs are too often in immediate view, and time after time people still cry out asking why nobody ever seems to have done anything.

Sometimes I wonder if it's just because people don't know what to do, and they might automatically presume it's not even worth thinking about with having no practical solution coming to mind.

But you know what I think our biggest downfall is in not tackling the many forms of the abuse that we see out there? Our attraction for things and security, and the overlooking of tribal factors that cause people to not want what is morally right for a group unit, but do anything to prevent what it may perceive as weakening it. If an abuser has bonded tightly with a group, or is a leader providing resources - many of the subconscious tribal factors may come into play without people even realising it.

That may well be the reason why so often those that have spotted an abuser with much clout in their community, even when going to other authorities with those concerns – those calls and concerns will often lead to absolutely nowhere.

One powerful mask sometimes used by those under the radar is the sense of kindness and charity. Strip much of it down and put all of the excuses into a bin bag, and essentially what you have left is a master of psychological manipulation.

Nobody really wants to be the bad guy, and when you're a person that has spotted something in which a whole group are in denial of, then it's all too easy to be labelled the troublemaker or an inconvenience, toxic and damaging, or an agent of destruction.

Those tackling the behaviour of such types are not only taking on the abuser, but the entire framework which other people have developed a tight sense of relying on for various different reasons.

Those having gone out of their way to expose such injustices and safeguard others around them are all too frequently left in not only mentally traumatic situations, but completely isolating ones too. Having reached out to many people around them out of desperation to be heard, things get understandably worse, and they become constantly shocked and frustrated at how little others seem to be caring about it, despite social media influencers garnering thousands or millions of viewers to talk about the same old celebrity abusers.

For such people, life becomes a feeling of having reality completely flipped upside-down. We all have our individually naiveties, but I think generally it's too easy to presume that people will stand up and be there when they're needed. For anyone thinking that I'm just talking waffle - why not yourselves go and ask those people that have been trying to shout it out for many years.

I don't mean money-machine internet forum groups, I'm talking about the people that cared purely from their own backs and weren't ever out in the first place to reel you in with dramatized stories where the internet cults gather, and which in many cases do very little to prevent another child having to go through it again.

There's no real point in simply shouting at our TV's and reposting the memes that we see online whilst also being in denial of how easily these things can and do slip by in front of our eyes and right over our heads. Without accepting that, none of our vents against paedophilia, reposting of hunter team stings or celebrity conspiracy theories count for anything at all. Just theatre, and something to pass the time and keep people feeling entertained - in my own opinion.

Perhaps upon thinking about this, it may reveal some aspects of why those like myself can easily end up becoming the scapegoat. Some can mistakenly look down on that as being somewhat of a pushover, but what it actually is – is the revelation of how well-engineered some people's worlds can be so that anyone else challenging it will be systemically belittled out of the situation and outcasted by the tribe. What seriously needs to be acknowledged though, is the admittance of when our thoughts and emotions are being completely exploited and manipulated to do so to others, not only on an individual and community level, but on a social and political one too.

Unfortunately, I can only remember all too well of witnessing what I thought had been an authentic and efficient safeguarding network be at complete odds with what I'd imagined.

For all of our exposes on cover-up scandals, what is often failed to be acknowledged are the intricate ins and outs of how not only the abuse itself gradually seeps into the fabric of an environment, but also the ways it gets systemically disregarded.

As we are finding out all too much these days, despite the great work, dedication and risk to personal safety of many police officers, the phenomenon of such treatment and disregarding of some within our society, even from within the force, is becoming all too apparent.

It's a crucial time currently for people to swallow their pride and find strength in facing the truths that we need to hear in which to move forward, instead of avoiding and interpreting such statements as a personal attack on one's ethics and abilities.

For any police officers that may find themselves reading this book, all I ask is can you imagine simply trying to be a good human and doing what you knew was right, only for almost everyone around you to simply treat you like you're being crazy or weird?

For some years it had felt that I'd even started to believe it, but deep down I know the sense of complete isolation was an illusion, and that this sense of being shut down and not taken seriously was happening to a lot more people than I'd first thought.

This particular event in my life had also brought with it some very harsh and dangerous realities too, but even all of that intense stuff aside, the mental health effects of feeling like the world has for no good reason completely turned against you is a situation that I'd never have imagined until being there.

If it wasn't for the fact that I'd further researched into things relating to my experiences and eventually found out that many more people were going through the exact same thing, then I honestly have no clue where my head would be at now. Looking back at it, I can honestly say that it felt a heartbreaking situation and one that I'd never want to see another person ever have to go through.

As if people like me ain't had that shit all of our lives anyway, except for now we've been reaching out to the people that have the capacity to change these things only to be too often so belittled. What gives me a strong faith though in continuing writing this book is now knowing that it's not simply all in my head like some would have you believe, and that such failings caused from misplaced perceptions of others have now hit a bottleneck.

I know I'm far from what a lot of people would consider a grass, or informant for those outside of the UK, but what police and authorities need to know about those like me in regards to us flagging up the most vulgar of crimes is that often the perception that those like myself won't be taken seriously is so prevalent that for us it doesn't take long to see the masks slipping from some of those around us, and the red flags to start appearing.

Perhaps those people know all too well how all of this works, and that the failings to tackle such things with no genuine appearance of care are so systemic that they feel they can simply continue to get away with it, and as some of you may have already sensed through video coverage of such events - the confidence is often all too brash.

However much I take my hat off to the many dedicated sting teams volunteering their time, personal safety and mental health to not only directly tackle online child grooming but also reveal the true scope of the phenomenon – unfortunately, despite such brilliant efforts in at least pointing us into the right direction - this is only the tip of the iceberg and often fails to reveal clearly how these things often operate more subtly and between the lines in the offline world, and in some cases with more seemingly intelligent people.

Still in many ways, in their credit - the hunter teams have hit a social information goldmine in the sense that for many decades, if not centuries or millennia - many people have often simply been needing that bit of proof to confirm their suspicions or act without being shut down by the world around them. Despite us always knowing that such things go on, the concept of it all being somewhat between the lines had for a long time become something society had got used to.

However, the many sting teams that have posted online the phenomenal amounts of paedophile stings as videos have done a fantastic job of revealing how under the surface, yet in plain sight all of this really is.

For those that have found themselves deep into the world of such research, it can be a lot to process and still leaves you with many questions such as - was it always like this? Or - has it risen significantly and got way out of control? Whatever is going on these are certainly revealing and transcending times in relation to what is potentially the awareness of major and en-mass social gaslighting - which has possibly been happening for thousands of years.

I would imagine though that truly dedicated sting teams see all too well the difference between those that support their work for the right reasons - and those which can sometimes be there as part of the circus, and see it as an opportunity to revel in mania and release their pent up frustrations.

Perhaps some of the police themselves know all too well that if the amount of people liking and sharing these videos were also spotting and reporting such events themselves - then those there to investigate it simply wouldn't cope with the workload.

However, despite the calls for a more efficient safeguarding system by what is now a rapidly growing natural and hard to tame movement, the fact such issues have been somewhat alternative and on the very fringes should be a clear sign in itself that we're still in the processes of truly acknowledging worlds in which we haven't quite had our eyes opened to fully yet.

The acknowledging and learning of those worlds is certainly not an easy journey, but for those currently navigating through them - what makes it much harder than it ever should be is knowing that there's such little support for most of the people going through it.

For all of our technological advances though - we find ourselves again at some sort of paradox at times when we automatically assume that efficient safeguards are in place and are ran by passionate and competent people.

Sadly, we're being proved wrong time and time again, in what has in some places become a psychopathic take-over. Many of us have had the misfortune of realising that those problems often come right from the top though, in which it only takes one covert psychopath to use their Machiavellian manipulation to secure influential positions - and before you know it the whole structure is dysfunctional, except that not everyone always recognizes it whilst it continues to give the illusion of a sense of efficiency.

It's too easy to assume in this era's too-often superficial world that everything seeming official does exactly what it makes out, and that anything reported to the authorities will lead to some sort of paper-trail that visibly beams out to everyone, when in reality there are too many people that find their concerns about abuse, stalking and child grooming often bizarrely going nowhere.

There are of course many other factors that cause such abuses and phenomena to go largely undetected. One reason may be that regarding abuse towards children and young people - perhaps we must acknowledge its varying levels and forms of sadism to truly understand why.

Whilst we're often looking out for the most obvious and vicious signs of abuse, perhaps sometimes those with the most long-term and devastating impacts are those which are played out so subtly that they not only start operating more in plain sight as time passes by, but can lead to people being victims or perpetrators for decades.

Despite the massive revelations of grooming scandals involving teenage girls in places such as Telford and Rotherham, and as well as the huge amounts that we now know relating to the abuse within the Catholic church, perhaps it's still often overlooked how particularly hard it can be for a young males to admit when they've been groomed or abused.

Even adults who refuse to become bystanders and attempt to take safeguarding actions to protect such young people can find themselves up against immediate barriers in doing so. Particularly when in the mind of a young male often the last thing many of them want is not only to be needlessly questioning their own sexuality, but also to have others - including their peers - misinterpreting it.

Not only that, but there could be something to be said about the huge failures to acknowledge the real scope of trauma in young people involved in abuse. Perhaps it's easy to forget that their calls of injustice are too often counteracted by questions from adults such as "Well, why did you go back there if they abused you?" and "Why didn't you say anything when it was happening?" which upon hearing such questions I can't help but see the disregard for what people are actually going through, however misplaced and unintentional it might be.

It's one of the very reasons that abuse scandals involving young males are only revealed all too often decades too late. Even if the world believes that young people are supported upon such a situation arising, often without words really needing to be spoken there is too often the more engrained message that even acknowledging when boundaries have been clearly broken that it will rock the boat too much and cause pain to those accused, often leading almost everybody to do nothing and wave events off as completely innocent events.

This is perhaps another thing easily overlooked that a lot of perpetrators likely know too well and take advantage of. In the eyes of a perpetrator it is another blessing in their eyes no doubt, but something that over time society is learning not only to acknowledge, but to successfully put those teachings of our failings into practice, something which is obviously taking more time than some of us would have hoped.

But it's not to say that I don't feel that the young women affected by other manifestations of abuse always have a voice either.

I've come to realise over time that I'm often guided towards those that have witnessed such scandals and a huge sense of neglect from society. But for all of the shocking news coverage and television documentaries regarding the abuse of girls and young women - there's no doubt that it's a positive thing for this be in the public conscience at least.

However, it's not like some of these young women aren't on social media these days sharing more of their stories and raising awareness, still few flock to them to hear it for themselves though, and instead many seem to want to hear the stories from self-proclaimed child protection activists recycling other peoples reporting and following the mob on Youtube.

Perhaps I'm just being inpatient though, and one day we'll actually start collectively putting the knowledge we've learned into doing the right thing offline and on ground level - and all start stepping up when we're needed to do so instead of being charmed by those that want you sleepwalking.

With these sorts of particular issues operating for so long under the surface, protecting its often cryptic status is something those currently abusing others are often so desperate to maintain.

Those newly discovering such worlds may not only have a mentally harrowing experience, but also a chaotic and dangerous one too.

I think it wouldn't be happening like that half as much though if there hadn't been a wide-open exploit in what is clearly a huge sign of human disconnection happening currently in our society.

With our dopamine receptors being hijacked almost every second of the day by one means or other, along with the stresses of simply making sure the bills are being paid, it's all too understandable that often there's little time for people to feel they can truly soak in the rest of the world around them.

But those without internet marketing suave, or not ticking the familiarity boxes know all too well of feeling that the majority of others remain completely silent and static when they've brought up these issues.

For others, simply caring and deciding to act upon instinct is something that becomes effortless to do, but often feels impossible in the end to make any actual meaningful change once the world has completely closed in on them. You should never give up though, and whenever you need to leave a trail of solid evidence, you just have to put your faith in God!

It's maybe also important to remember that most people don't intentionally become bystanders. Accepting that we've all had moments where something has gone right over our head and only come to us after, or that we really wished afterwards that we'd have acted on something when we'd failed to do so is all part of the healing process. Instead of feeling too much shame or guilt about it - instead it should be taken as a hard-hitting lesson that has taught us the consequences of failing to be as a sharp as we would have liked.

Unfortunately, the things that I've spoken about above are only the immediate barriers in seeking any sort of justice in regard to the protection of children and young people. Having no background in clinical psychology or training in mental disorders I'm not going to claim to have any suggestions for how the courts and criminal justice system can efficiently be used to eradicate such a phenomenom.

That question in itself can bring about many mixed emotions and painful feelings for those that have in any way been affected by such things. This is why when I do see an abuse topic trending and hear certain statements of what some people would do to the perpetrator - to much degree it's easy to fully sympathise with how much an event has truly pierced someone's heart.

Nevertheless, among those calling out for the most extreme of punishments in some cases, it's important to see clearly who is really meaning what they're saying and why. To those most hurt and bruised because of such things - there's a natural reply to let them know that we fully understand their feelings. But other human dynamics can cause people to get drawn in by the chaos, eventually causing the real messages and overall sense of true understanding to be skewed - and thus becoming a groupthink back-patting and popularity contest, as well as a place for some people to simply reveal their more sadistic side.

But for those that have found themselves on this journey not through conspiracy websites or trending topics - but through direct on-the-ground experience, for all the ways some of those people may feel that they've fell back somewhat slightly in society, there's also something to be said about how severely underestimated and undervalued such life experience is.

There are many people from backgrounds like myself that when spotting a predatory danger would often react in an instant. Perhaps some of us aren't always able to describe such a complex situation so articulately to others, but it's all from a much deeper learnt instinct anyway.

But what a lot of those people are crying out for is for the authorities that are there to prevent the worst of abuses to have that same fire in their bellies against it, which as we are still learning has too often not been the case.

Perhaps it's time for the world to move on from being hoodwinked by sickly-sweet portrayals of charity and self-righteousness. Despite the appearance of obvious mental health issues from some of those affected most, maybe more people will eventually see some of those people's rage and mental state for what it really is, a perfectly natural reaction to a systemic problem, instead of simply labelling them as anti-social or crazy.

But carelessly ushering those people into those sorts of boxes seems to be merely the easy way out for what has far too long been a mass cover up, and despite all of the pretence - a continuation of failing to want to improve on our own aspects of social understanding.

Chapter Nine – Finding Faith

For those that get it, or for those frequently in the pits of despair themselves, perhaps it's easy enough to imagine yourself standing there whilst raising your arms up with facing palms open. "What the heck is going on? Are you serious? This can't be for real!" you shout.

However, that's the reality for many people in a society where we're all still currently ironing out our societal issues. Perhaps on a bigger level we'll make some positive use from the many recent tragic and systemic failings that have come to light over recent years, instead of it being just something that we talk about one morning at the breakfast table after it's been on the news.

Even the crown court case at Southwark had brought up past encounters with the police that I'd completely forgotten about. Back when I was sixteen and waiting outside of the homeless day centre that I'd go to in Charing Cross - one time two plain clothes police officers had pulled me up to search me for no real reason apart from presumably hoping that it would lead to an arrest. I'd instantly protested it at the time, letting the officers know that it was blatant harassment.

So, in typical Ben fashion straight to the police station I went, somewhat furious that I was being treated in such a way, and in all the credit to the chief of the station, he immediately brought me in to a room to have a chat.

He laid out clearly my two options, I could either make an official complaint in which there'd be a whole internal process and the officer could find himself up for suspension, or that he could simply have a word with him and let him know that it wasn't to happen again.

With my frustrations been genuine, and simply feeling that it shouldn't have happened I went with what I'd felt had been the more productive option, and thanked the chief superintendent in advance for having words with the officer. Did I really want to go through a whole legal process because of one stop and search? Not really – I was a sixteen-year-old lad with much more interesting things to do.

Having almost completely forgotten about that incident - to my surprise it had been brought up in the crown court trial over a decade later as a counter-claim to the officers defence that I was simply being cold and vicious by testifying against them.

It was a good move by the detective sergeant that had investigated them in a trial where I'd had everything thrown at me by the defence to try and paint me as a troublesome anti-authoritarian that 'had it in for the police'.

They'd even gone through all of my Youtube videos and targeted one in particular where I'd pretended to be an elf character called Terrence, in which I'd the sped the video up to make it appear that he was moving faster and speaking in a higher pitch. In that particular sketch 'Terrence' was making light of being stopped and searched by the police, which I'm sure you can gather by now was something I'd been going through a lot growing up in London.

"Did you, or did you not say in this particular video that the police didn't realise who they were fucking with?" questioned their barrister in a scowling tone. I had to explain to the court that the entire sketch was satire and that I'd go on to immediately say that it was because the elf was going to piss in the police officer's whisky on Christmas evening, and it was in no relation whatsoever to those particular officers. I suppose it goes to show exactly how much they were clutching at straws towards the end of the trial.

But considering what had initially been a victory back then, I still have to acknowledge the many ways in which I've been extremely fortunate. I could have easily not had a voice recorder or be unable to prove the truth, or in even more tragic cases that could have been me restrained with no real sense of care, resulting in serious injury or my death.

The memory from being sixteen in Charing Cross has also brought up other memories from my younger days, and yet other examples of witnessing what should be concerning information that seems to go right over people's heads.

See, for too long it's felt that the world has been trying to convince me that it's weird for caring in the way that I do about it. Whilst curtain-twitchers and small-time snitchers make reports about matters which a lot of us see as needless child's play, those which genuinely go out of their way to prevent harm to others are rarely even listened to. There is simply yet more tragic "hello, is there anybody in there?" moments. A clear disconnection.

I remember all too well walking into the same police station all of those years ago, when it had been common hearsay from local homeless people that some were going missing for months on end after being offered work but getting completely exploited. F fair few homeless people from the west end weren't getting paid and would find themselves completely stuck in the middle of nowhere.

I'd noticed the crew that were picking them up were currently back in the area looking for homeless people to recruit. Despite trying to raise the alarm it had become just another wasted effort though and simply the ever-repeating pattern of my life – the shaking head asking what the heck their supposed to do about anything, and me walking out of a station completely confused with reality and wondering what planet I'm even on.

It is only recently through hearing other voices in the public arena that I've felt I can even write this book. There's been a lot holding me back from sharing many of my experiences for years now, and a huge part of that is social peer-pressure and worrying what others will think about me and judging me as a bit crazy. How much real time and connection have I really wasted because of that though? No messing about anymore. Boooosh!

Not too long ago though, yet another theme of feeling that those from backgrounds like myself are seen as somewhat irrelevant in society had surfaced unexpectedly when reflecting one day on an event from my childhood that those of you that have read *Poems From a Runaway* may be familiar with.

Having written about being held up with a sword and locked in a flat by a grown man at twelve years old in Edmonton Green - it was only recently after years since writing about it in the book that I even began to realise how little I remember of any real investigation at all, despite the story coming out to all of the staff in the children's home and even filtering through to my dad.

I'm not even sure if my own mind is playing tricks on me when I think I remember explaining my story briefly to a policeman. Despite that, it seemed that no further questions were asked.

I guess I'd always imagined people would do all that they could to secure a conviction regarding such a crime. But as far as I can remember there were no other conversations about it, no photos ever shown to me to ask me if I recognised any buildings or streets, and it appeared to have been completely forgotten about.

Upon realising it, it certainly brought up some intense feelings and questions. Why can't I remember police officers urging me to provide them more detailed information? And why was there no sense of urgency that they had to stop such a person in their tracks?

I'm aware that it's all too easy to look at someone else's job and not understand the nuts and bolts of their work and the many unseen tasks involved. Still though, despite still being in the search for finding answers as to exactly what did happen regarding all of this, I can't help feeling that if the police did have more urgency in acting back then, considering the amount of CCTV even all of those years ago I'd put my money on the fact that securing a conviction could have been possible.

Even if it wasn't, perhaps the simple ethos of wanting to protect children and young people should have been a priority.

I can't help but wonder if perhaps the authorities felt that it was all completely from my own doing. Holding that ethos though simply denies the true realities of not only complex life and family dynamics, but also of the fact that so many children and young people go missing, and for many different reasons.

Although this might sound condescending to some, I can only feel that perhaps holding such youth in this regard is a sign of still needing to reach certain levels of emotional maturity which can not only influence some individuals, but if they are the ones in key positions then whole structures within society.

It's not all doom and gloom though, and as I've mentioned before and likely will do again, I think we're certainly in very interesting and turbulent times at the moment regarding social change.

Despite the beat-down tone from many that things will simply never change, it's important to remember that there are still those within the structures of our society doing what they can to achieve some sort of progress, despite its challenges.

For most of them some sort of painful experience or hundred has led to them developing a strong sense of conscience and following their heart, others finding themselves in somewhat influential professional roles are simply rare breeds that perhaps don't come around all that often.

Initially, my frustrations relating to my kidnapping as a kid brought up much anxiety and feelings of psychosis, and not even from the event itself. Perhaps not immediately, but after realising after twenty-five years what I think is the fact that there was no real investigation into it - I couldn't help but wonder if I should at least have made some sort of report, and so I did.

Not that I've ever expected the police to suddenly drop all of their things and assist with me, especially after so long, and nor had I really expected them to secure any sort of conviction. But I suppose that it's just what I'd expected from policing in regard to child protection, and that these sorts of things are at least looked into and noted in the case that they're connected with anything else or could prevent any further abuses.

I was told that because I was now living outside of London, as well as my home county that I was missing from at the time, that they'd be sending some officers from the local force to come and speak with me. However, after over a year waiting I hadn't heard a thing, which had severely offset my mental health in turn causing my anxiety to turn into a sudden wave of rage, and possibly to the point of psychosis.

It had in fact led to what I can only describe now as a situation that I'm somewhat embarrassed about, but also hold some self-forgiveness in the fact that I'm only human. Silly me hadn't written down any crime number or names of any of the officers had I, and after it sounding quite certain that someone was about to come and speak to me, along with the feelings brought up of experiences relating to other police failings of child protection I'd then lost the plot outside of the station – in turn leading me to shout up to them that they didn't care about children and that people were getting sick of it.

As expected, it would lead to concerned and baffled looks from those within the station, but had resulted in one police officer opening up the window before then coming down to talk to me, in which I'd explained the situation as well as apologising for my manic outburst.

She briefly noted down the basics of the story and said that she'd be back in touch with me later that day after completing some other tasks, but as I'd half-expected because of an ever-repeating pattern that was the last I'd ever heard from her.

At the time of writing this book however, I'm pleased to say that I've been blessed with the opportunity to connect with certain people that are able to help shape the change within policing that many of us know is desperately needed.

It might be a long road, but hopefully the more of us that speak out about these sorts of systemic problems and are fortunate enough for that to somehow get heard, then the less people will be convinced by their own false-perceptions of how these sorts of things actually play out in the real world.

In many ways I'm fortunate to have come across those I sense a warmth from in regards to understanding my feelings and mental health effects towards such circumstances. Life has indeed revealed to me the many challenges that well-meaning police officers may face even within their own professional structures regarding a sense of healthy social connection and how they police crimes of abuse.

Fortunately, the problems are actually starting to reveal now much more vividly in the public conscience. Still though, I can't help but feel for those that have been witnessing such failures for many years, especially those like myself that went on to experience such detrimental mental health effects and were led to believe that they were the ones with the problem, which for most can be a completely shattering experience.

These current times bring much opportunity for self-healing for many of those people like myself. Despite all of those moments that people have felt like their sense of reality has been turned completely upside down, and for the amount of people turning their backs on them - finally now the rejection of our experiences and concerns are being spoken of directly by those wanting a more meaningful change in safeguarding and policing.

Chapter Ten – Getting Too Freaky

I think it should be only understandable that over the last few years there's been a lot of people struggling to make sense of some of their experiences. Even what I've written so far doesn't reflect truly the frequency of bizarre events that some people have found themselves going through, which in turn lead to severe mental health effects.

For those that find themselves in such a hellish sense of reality, it can be a genuine struggle at times to process exactly where the sources of abuse are coming from. That's to no discredit of anybody going through such things, but it can take many years for some of us to figure out when the abuse is happening on various different levels.

I think perhaps what mental health professionals need to take into account and feel that many don't currently, is that it can only take a short series of such bombardments of baffling and intense circumstances to really affect someone's mental health for the long term.

Instead of simply labelling somebody as psychotic or schizophrenic, would it not be more authentic and healthy to help them understand and make sense of their experiences instead?

I know that I certainly don't have to worry that I'm giving away any tricks to those that may exploit them here, as the people knowing this know all too well on completely different levels exactly what they're doing.

One thing that I learned deeply as a kid living on the streets is exactly how clued up predatory and abusive people can be in reading people. More so than most in fact, and to the point where many can smell in an instant if you're the type of person that society has tossed aside, or if you've taken a beating from life. Whilst the rest of the world passes by and often fails to acknowledge such people, those wishing to exploit, use or abuse them can often smell them a mile away like a shark in water.

In many ways thinking about all of this makes me sympathise with what I think of as the overlooked factors regarding racism, homophobia and other experiences of frequent prejudice and abuse. Despite the fact that we know some people are treated differently, have we ever taken the time to wonder what it's like when it's happening constantly, and time and time again.

Many simply become baffled, broken and confused - and despite there always being individuals and groups making a stand and shouting things out in a rational and articulate way, there are often many more walking various roads in their quests for answers in what they might not realise is simply systemic abuse.

Whilst in a state of confusion when processing surprising and memorable events, sometimes one after the other, seeking support from a world that often shrugs its shoulders can and does lead some people down other rabbit holes whilst searching for answers on the internet.

Thankfully, there's been a recent surge over the last few years of well-intended and educated folk raising awareness about the nuts and bolts of psychopathy and narcissism. Before then though, and still affecting many people to some degree is the consideration of the options they may come across in internet forums - where unknown to them they are sometimes being further manipulated, exploited and abused.

This can lead people searching for what really are very simply answers, but without such information about behavioural disorders such as psychopathy, sadism and narcissism, those particularly in their younger years of life and without well-intentioned guidance can find themselves easily sucked into the world of paranoid conspiracy theories which although at times may hint at stories of truth - are simply too often twisted to enhance the drama and shock value of a particular issue.

This does little for those who find themselves time and time again in complete baffling situations. I guess it's easy for any of us to forget how prevalent the abuse can be in society, even visits to the dentists have left me with an extreme trauma of going back when feeling that mistakes or simple incompetence which led to further issues in fact being clear acts of sadism.

That's how prevalent all this messed up stuff is, and despite it being so easy to overlook - I think these times are teaching us to finally take notice of those limited moments which can reveal the tip of the iceberg, and teach us to step up and do the right thing to prevent it, whether you're a worker on the ground, a team manager or the boss.

Currently though, in the field of mental health and psychiatry - I don't feel that the true scope of abuse is counted for, which in turn leads people that are absolutely desperate for support and answers to feel further misunderstood, and mislabelled as simply crazy, irrational or fantasists.

What certainly doesn't help though is when those from impoverished and crime-stricken areas are witnessing real-life situations that those living life fairly well-protected from simply can't comprehend. Those with any stories of exploitation, gaslighting, stalking or harassment that have happened either on the ground or through manipulation of technological devices too -often see their experiences completely disregarded, both by those that naturally gravitate towards abuse and those who have been somewhat a little fortunate to have not lived with significant levels of it as yet.

Perhaps even the initial neglect shown towards some of our more fragile and sensitive people in society has been one of the factors into pushing them further down a path of confusion and delusion. In many ways I feel that here we are judging some of these people for their distorted sense of reality, yet what really have we done to help guide them back to a grounded sense of understanding?

That's all some of those people out there needed that we now label as too far gone, just someone to listen to and connect with to help them fully understand the world and their experiences from a genuinely life-educated outlook.

When things involve technological harassment and the manipulation of devices connected to the internet or with radio frequencies then it's a completely dark trip for those feeling isolated in a world that so often denies that this sort of thing even exists, yet at the same time you can find out to manipulate somebody's devices simply searching it on Youtube.

Devices switching on and off, and clear obvious disruptions are just a small number of events that somebody using their computer frequently or working on a project will notice but find it hard to express or be believed.

It's all too easy for others to blame these things on glitches, but when you're the one noticing the extremely odd conveniences which cause

saboutage to your work whilst internet connections get mysteriously
disabled during certain events, or even full-on coincidental computer
crashes - then it becomes a somewhat draining experience.

Despite scope for misreading a situation or of there being paranoia or
anxiety, only the person experiencing it truly knows and feels what is
actually happening, but the trauma from such harassment and abuse in
itself causes various degrees of further paranoia, and for the person
experiencing it to also start jumping too quickly to conclusions.

But for those that are quick to dismiss such claims as simply getting
things wrong or being completely paranoid, perhaps it's important to
remember that technological abuse and harassment has been around
for much longer than smartphones and the internet has. Back in the
day when people were using their landlines even then people were
getting 'trolled' so to speak. Also, with the invention of the CB radio
came a whole host of scanners which had eventually ended up on
some of the council estates of Great Britain. I should know, my nan
had one!

I remember clearly one day as a teenager upon visiting her whilst back
in the midlands, and when messing around with the scanner at the
time I'd presumed that it could only pick up signals from CB radios.
Even though mobile phones hadn't been around that many years, I
remember one day overhearing what I was a certain was a mobile
phone call, and with there being a button on the scanner to talk, I
could have used, but can't remember if I ever did.

If only I'd remembered all of that a decade or so on when I'd being
getting trolled through what had been quite a basic mobile phone,
which although could technically connect to the internet - it wasn't at
all really worth using it for back then to be honest.

It was a rough time for me back then though, and one that had
consisted of many odd and strange events, but during that particular

period there'd been some frequent interruption of my phone calls whilst standing outside of the squat that I'd been living in.

During one particular call I'd been getting people making some sort of demonic sounding shouting noises which were so weird that despite wishing I'd simply been wise enough to forget about it, it lived rent-free in my head for quite some time.

There'd been a few other weird events like that too, but whoever it was had been at it again during another phone call when all of a sudden I heard what appeared to be the sounds of a child's toy.

At the time my mind had tried to form some sort of rational logic when I said over the call that I was on "Oh it's just some cross-over from a baby monitor or something" in which immediately the keyboard that I'd heard playing sounds was now being played by what was obviously not a child, and was someone that knew how to play music - and quite skillfully too, in which I couldn't help but feel that it was adult and that something wasn't quite right.

There were a lot of answers that I was searching for at the time, and not knowing who was doing it had planted some major suspicions in my mind about the people that I was living with and had completely freaked me out, although I'm hoping that it was one of the neighbours in the nearby flats or across the road.

It shouldn't feel like a risk to feel crazy disclosing this, but what puts me at ease apart from the memory of the scanner at my nans place is when during one of my many times researching into this subject I came across a video - which if I remember right was from Sky News Australia, where a woman was going through almost the exact same experience that I had been, with people screaming demonic sounds down her phone and seeing with her own eyes her devices being manipulated.

It's a tough place to be until others around you acknowledge it because it can simply appear to sound too crazy, which is why I've never really spoken much about it to anyone.

It's a strange set of circumstances to be in for those going through it though because despite their being so much information about hacking and stalking, I think it's very much still a taboo subject for anybody to talk about because there can be so much doubt in various minds involved.

In today's world - internet technology is everywhere. Similarly to peadophilia, perhaps this form of abuse is one of those issues that has been brushed under the carpet and denied of acknowledgement for so long that it's led to a dark underbelly that can thrive and breed out of control.

"Oh you're just being paranoid" is a simple statement that has worked wonders to help cover up abuse scandals over the many years, and although I'm more than aware of both the obviously damaged people and also the Walter Mitty's that find themselves telling the world on online forums that the CIA are beaming voice messages into their skull and whatnot, I'm not doubting the possibility of any more completely shocking revelations to society.

But even there, just then, my immediate judgement that such people are simply damaged or creating a narrative instead of considering if they've simply gone way off track and are experiencing the further effects of trauma from it is perhaps something to be acknowledged. I guess we all judge and need to think about things a little deeper sometimes.

It's no surprise though that in a world where so many are going through an experience of struggling to understand why people are treating others the way that they do, that some among us when in their quest for answers come across various internet themes such as 'gangstalking' and organized harassment.

It's something I'd personally began looking at in my younger years around the time of all of the weird phone stuff, but there were other events triggering it too, in which it became hard to trust anyone and know who was really on my side.

I was a care-free spirit back then to much degree, but for all of my claims of being street-wise and often being one step ahead of those out to hold me back, perhaps it's time to finally admit that there's just something about me that beams out 'easy target'. Not that it always leads to me becoming a victim by any means, but perhaps I'm just simply one of those people that everyone wants to have a pop at.

Having being brought into a crew that were making raves in warehouses not long before my freaky sets of events, as well as myself veering into the anti-war movement, perhaps there were specific reasons that those things were happening to me. Had I been part of some sort of campaign or investigation that I hadn't been aware of at the time? Or were darker forces simply trying to disrupt the light and good vibes from the parties? It would have certainly made more sense of some of my other times in London where I'd keep noticing some of the same specific faces all over the place.

On a less stalkey note though, and a much brighter one, sometimes that's just London. Still though... ya know.

With everything combined, including constantly being stopped and searched outside the squat that I was living in during our early days there, before I knew it I'd found myself deep into the world of MK Ultra, Cointelpro and a whole host of masonic conspiracies.

Whatever was going on, I was now living life in a dark state of mind of feeling watched and monitored. Was it the police doing all this to me? Was it the freemasons as I'd read in some of the research? Were any of my friends in on it even? Or were darker forces trying to divide us?

Not that I even knew anything about the Mason's in all fairness, but something about my life at the time started to feel very mysterious, but with those goings on it all had somewhat of a dark edge.

As you can imagine, it's not the most peaceful and enlightening of times when your heads stuck in all of that.

There's no other worse feeling though than being completely alone when you're trying to talk to professionals about such things in regards to technological trolling. Perhaps it goes to show that generally we just need that boost in connection that actually reaches out a hand and helps provide rational answers to people that might not have a single soul providing them any real wholesome and grounding insight into what is actually happening.

So, is that really a mental disorder? Or merely the symptom of a society still in need of its search for a much deeper connection with itself?

Who's to say that such organized cults don't exist anyway. For all of my dismissal of such things, perhaps if anything the recent revelations through hunter teams and online media has only brought me more questions than answers such as – if this is what people are prepared to do to kids then what are they doing to adults? And what if there really is some well-organized dark web cult or something which through unseen abuse of various forms gets its thrills from seeing the demise and destruction of someone?

For all of my conspiratorial thinking, despite having a different opinion years ago, I fear that for some that it might not be too far off the mark anymore to be honest.

Still though, largely I put it down to simply being an unguided self-learner in a world where abuse has its many ways of operating completely under the radar and making sure that it often gets doubted

- leading it to become an all-too tempting phenomenon to partake in for many.

I've gotten used to my devices going weird all year during the time of writing this book, and the source of it has been impossible for me to answer although I have my suspicions. But the quest for answers speaks for itself about how much confusion and chaos it can bring to someone's life, as well as ripping apart relationships and families. Sadly, I fear that it's currently completely unacknowledged and the people involved are often feeling so isolated that it's simply being left to breed.

If there's one thing that I think people can do to help prevent such confusion happening to others, then it's by introducing the concepts and leanings of psychopathy and narcissism to students at a certain age, perhaps during one free-schedule day near the end of term or something for older teenagers.

Sure, kids already know in their own ways when someone's being damaging or toxic, but similarly to journeys that I've previously mentioned in this book, perhaps both young people and adults need to sometimes learn what they already know from a completely different perspective in order to gain a more rounded sense of insight.

If anything, it can give more clarity of instinct, which is quite empowering for the many people that are gaslit into doubting their own gut-feelings.

Of course, anyone considering such an approach must do so with fairness, balance and caution. It simply wouldn't be productive, healthy or genuinely connective to inspire young people to go on a narcissist witch hunt, but instead perhaps we should rebuild a framework that not only inspires young people to immediately and naturally challenge such behaviours, but also provide genuine support and outlets for people battling with these types of personality disorders without getting manipulated.

It is the sort of thing that we presume is already there within our mental health system, but to what degree? And is it even really working? Those of us that are concerned that certain aspects of narcissism and sadism may well be on the rise would certainly question otherwise.

Chapter Eleven – The things they all presume

As mentioned already in this book, I genuinely believe that there's many forms of stigma and presumptions that those such as myself experience on a frequent basis, whether that's because of my shaggy dreadlocks or my unfamiliar eyes-wide open care-free bounce-walk, or sometimes it's simply because I've opened up about my past as a runaway kid living on the streets.

Despite witnessing it for most of my life, I've still always found it surprising at what sorts of presumptions people will instantly make about myself after hearing snippets of my life story.

Perhaps more people need to remember that not all of us are cut out for some of the current social themes and trends in which we start photoshopping our lives in order to market ourselves, our work and our creations.

Unfortunately, it seems to be the world that some of us are getting used to, in which those like myself that don't always fit into those sorts of boxes, nor really want to, remember a more authentic sense of social connection and are hoping that it's merely just a passing age.

When some people hear about our life experiences, especially our more extreme ones, then it can be really hard to convince them that there's anything else going about you at all.

I think people can easily forget that just because someone's been in some sort of tough or tragic position at some point in life, that actually these people have many more memories, experiences and dreams than some others give them the slightest bit of credit for. Another easy way for some to pick a scapegoat I suppose.

As for those among us that have found themselves battling with addictions - it's another complex situation and all too often a misunderstood one that gives no regard at times for the pain and weight that people are carrying and attempting to escape, or in some cases simply finding a state in which it doesn't prevent them from functioning in the everyday world.

Despite how easy it can be to look down on that - perhaps the big taboo is that so many people have such of a lack of support that it might even feel like their only option of continuing for another day. But whether you have addictions or not, people will often presume it anyway if they've heard that you've been homeless, even if it was some years ago - and more so if you have any sort of severe cognitive disabilities or impairments which can make you appear at times as if in other mental states.

I really feel for those people whose disabilities are mistaken as such, because knowing the amount of stigma and assumptions often made - I fear that they don't really stand a chance in life having already obviously been in a position that beams out that they don't have anyone to support them and are an immediate target of exploitation.

Apart from a small number of fantastic people and schemes that are helping those that have found themselves somewhat trapped on the fringes, and apart from a whole load more groups and cults that exploit vulnerable people into all sorts - more often than not it seems that the only time there's a concept of revealing the nuts and bolts of such a life where those people are noticed is when they become 'profitable content' or when an organisation wants to pat itself on the back in front of the rest of the world.

Still though, rarely we see the real journeys which reveal the actual attitudes and challenges some people face when trying to get opportunities that most of their peers find much easier. Perhaps both these film makes and organisations actually are doing some genuinely great work, but I can see gradually the temptation for us all to get sucked into a world of marketing that only continues to promote the two-dimensional understandings of life.

Whilst it can all too easily seem like anyone finding themselves homeless can simply go and get whatever support that they need, as the real world plays out the reality for some in regards to feeling a genuine sense of inclusion is realising that their experiences haven't been translated to the frequency a lot of people are used to hearing, essentially creating two completely different stories among peoples differing perceptions.

It doesn't matter how socially inclusive or confident you are, or how much you hold your arms open and welcome in the world, when you're going about life having experiences that a lot of people don't talk about enough to each other then it becomes a real challenge at times to feel understood by anyone at all.

It's a real shame that it's happening because that sense of separation deep down is all just an illusion anyway, but if only we'd seen those people living lives that we've felt unfamiliar with and saw not just our differences, but the real core things that we share and have in common.

Unfortunately, one of those things is that it seems as each day passes - the disregard, lack of willing connection and abuse that what we've been trying to get people to listen to for years has seeped more and more into mainstream reality, thankfully one of the only positives for us is that we don't have to sound crazy talking about it anymore.

Even after writing *Poems From a Runaway* and connecting with a whole community of others that were in the care system - I still hadn't realised until recently on a real deep level the stigmas associated with it, despite unknowingly experiencing some of them for all of my life.

Perhaps the signs should have been all too obvious of how things played out on much deeper levels when hearing those automatic presumptions about children in care being there because of behavioural issues or whatnot, which never does much to allow the deeper dynamics of an individual's story to be heard. Despite those things not always being spoken with words, those presumptions still get processed in the mind, and played out into responses, decisions and actions. Subconsciously at times even too.

"Oi you snowflake!" I hear some of you shout. Just wait though, maybe you're not thinking about this thoroughly enough.

"Sticks and stones may break my bones, but ignorance and prejudice completely get in the way of my life opportunities, and make me feel like I'm at the back of the queue."

Like I said before, living a life where you feel people are looking at anything but your true self is another thing that over time can not only smash a person's confidence, but lead them onto a completely new path of attempted entrepreneurship. Some of us try our best to do something legit, often struggling, whilst others choose crime. Often it

makes the difference between eating on one day, paying your phone
or internet bill, or having milk in your cup of tea.

And really, I suppose the purpose of this book in its entirety is to say
"hey people, why aren't we looking at the deeper things in life?"

I suppose though, part of that problem is within myself. Not that it's a
factor that I think particularly needs to be considered relating to such
stigma, but what I think a lot of people don't understand is that there
are many like me that have had to build our world and sense of reality
around a completely different base to those from stable and solid
family backgrounds.

It's no surprise that we develop our quirks and are often searching for
something to fill that big hole in our closest relationships, from my
perspective at least. Sometimes I imagine that those with more tighter
and solid families that they are naturally welcomed into , it's easier to
be content.

But if it's not masking the malfunctioning pain with drugs or escapism
through alcohol, then some of us find ourselves searching in many
other directions, ploughing ourselves into creative projects and the
like. Not that some medicinal elements hadn't played a part in helping
to provide a somewhat brighter and deeper tone to certain inner
bruises that I had, but perhaps a soother from feeling like some sort of
a freak and punchbag to society that doesn't come with any sore sense
of victimhood, but instead just an aching and confused feeling of
isolation that bred most in those times where I'd lacked a sense of
spiritual connection.

Similarly to the anxieties and paranoias that can come from some of
the things that I've mentioned previously, such people can be left
wondering what forces are really at play here and how some people
can feel so absolutely alien and irrelevant in many seemingly normal
worlds that they find themselves in, even if they've approached it with
nothing but genuine competence and confidence.

I've noticed that there seems to be the ethos that people have a lot of respect for such people with success stories, but ironically the actual journey in itself can be a completely different ballgame and if people aren't too aware of the vampire-like or selfish energies around them then they can find themselves being set up to fail.

What those that have been fortunate to not experience such challenges often don't understand is that it's not like some of these people even had the time or support to think about or process many of their life events either, which can leave obvious signs of wear and tear.

Such a person can be completely misunderstood from exterior perceptions, and when that happens in environments such as the workplace and also happen a lot - then these things can have an immediate impact on a person's life.

Ironically, often the former homeless person is completely underestimated regarding ethics, ability to fulfil a role well, and even at times doubts of their physical strength. The head-patting view that those struggling in certain aspects of life must be completely incompetent with everything else is all too self-soothing for those that choose to think it in a world that is often in denial of how deceived it can be by appearances.

In many ways, those with rougher edges can sometimes be a true test for others to see how deep one really looks to see and connect. Just saying.

I suppose I can find some sense of relief and understanding in knowing that anyone that can see the difference between natural drive and simply flexing knows exactly what I'm talking about. But the unintentional talking down and presumption that a person with experience of homelessness or mental health wouldn't be able to handle certain tasks is a constant barrier that I face whether in active employment or when seeking it.

At times it can bring a good feeling to such people when surprising colleagues and employers upon proving their prejudices otherwise. But as I mentioned earlier, some others simply can't handle it, and then before you know it you've got a shit-ton of needless drama that you've got to deal with once again, and often in such situations no matter what you do you either get stitched up and driven out, or you eventually just leave voluntarily because you've learned no matter what you do you just can't win.

But the one big question I ask though is this – are we as a society missing out greatly on certain dynamics which bring diversity and a wider perspective to groups, projects, places of employment and even politics by constantly disregarding the ideas, thoughts and experiences of those from backgrounds like myself?

Why shouldn't those coming from isolating life-circumstances feel like they've got something valuable or unique to bring to the table?

Sure, some of us see the world a little differently to what many are used to, but thanks to some good folk out there, they remind us that we shouldn't have to feel that we're weird or strange for being a little less cookie-cut like some have us believe, in which some just struggle to understand that it's how we've adapted to the turbulent lives that we've lived.

Having those ideas, thoughts and experiences unaccounted for in so many environments could be seen by some as a scandal even, something that society has failed to acknowledge for many years and perhaps one day, in some era, there will be that genuine earthly connection again where everyone is understood not through a misplaced perception on aesthetics, but for the more general and common human experience.

Not everybody is perfect, and mental health certainly does show it's symptoms on some of us, causing a bit of wear and tear. But perhaps the unspoken element here really is that despite a surge in technological advancement, that our spiritual advancement can be seen as primitive at times.

Sure, we all have fleeting moments of life bringing something special to the table, but can we not be honest with ourselves here for once and ask that when we do see people with such wear and tear, do we generally connect with them - or are they instantly targeted in one form or another as an opportunity to be exploited?

Perhaps the unnerving truth that is currently in the process of revealing itself is that all too often it's sadly the latter.

It's the sign of a society that shoots itself in the foot. Sure, it plays along and brushes its dirt under the carpets, but the signs of its failures and damage manifest in many forms that are all too easy for people to completely disregard.

Nobody really wants to admit that the heroin addict, the criminal, the obvious psychotic screaming to themselves down the street, or the passed out drunk in the doorway has any connection at all with the reality in which the observer sees it from, but those are just the more extreme and obvious symptoms of the disconnection disease. Accepting that we've far from nailed being a kind and civil society is something which strong heads are speaking up about at this point in time, and for all of our narcissistic self back-patting - many of us are finally starting to accept it.

It's been all too easy up until this point to simply tell someone to take responsibility for their lives in a culture that doesn't currently make it easy to do so. Perhaps this book really will help in its own way to more discussion about such prejudice, and if it helps one single person simply have people connect with them on a much deeper and genuine level then bish, bash, bosh. Job done.

Chapter Twelve – Kai the hitchhiker

As featured in Philip Fairbanks's book 'Smash, Smash, Smash: The True Story Of Kai The Hitchhiker'

Note to reader: Please visit my website for updates on Kai's legal situation.

As well as a lot of my personal experiences being what has inspired me to write this book - it has to be said that another one of the motivating factors in putting all of this together was rediscovering the injustices within a story of someone over in the United States that many of you might be familiar with, a guy known as Kai the hitchhiker... 'straight outta Dogtown.'

Named Caleb at birth - Kai's the name that he'd chosen to go by whilst on his journey through life, but he'd also been coined in the media as Kai 'the hatchet wielding' hitchhiker, which certainly doesn't do him or his story any real justice. But being able to take a deeper look at his story has been a great opportunity to reflect a little more on the experiences and stigmas that many people from the care system or going on to find themselves homeless may go on to face.

It's fair to say that if I hadn't of contacted Kai to get his permission to write about him in this book then what I'd have published from what I thought I'd learned from the Netflix documentary likely wouldn't have done his story any justice either.

Having analysed the documentary which had led to many of my own reflections on how others can perceive homelessness - I'd written this chapter, and there I was, convinced that I'd been advocating for him - but it wasn't until our communications when writing this book that he was able to correct a few statements that like many I'd been led to presume.

I guess it feels a somewhat privileged position to be in to be able to provide a much deeper angle to his story than I'd imagined when writing this book. Thanks to him putting me right on a few things I've had to re-write this chapter a few times, but I suppose anyone can copy and paste or rewrite a certain narrative. Not my style though.

Until recent years, Kai was known across the world after hitching a ride in California whilst homeless - when the driver of the car that he was in had rammed it into a group of workers, crushing one man to death. What had made Kai famous however was the unforgettable TV news report where upon being asked about what had happened during the event he'd described how the well-built owner of the vehicle was going psychotic and starting to attack others, and so Kai memorably went on in what seemed in bright yet fearless fashion to explain how he'd hit the man over the head several times with a hatchet that he had in his bag to stop him attacking the other people there.

Upon hearing such a story in fine detail - for most it would likely make one close their eyes and suck in a breath at what can seem harrowing. However, the fact that he'd just been in such a situation was far from apparent to most as he went on to speak in his TV news interview interrupting his description of the event with a message to those watching it to love and embrace the self-value in themselves whoever they were.

For a lot of people though, it was the way that he'd described fending off the attacker that had brought much more media attention and humour to the situation - in which the quote that he'd used - "Smash, Smash , Sm-aaash" - had become a popular internet meme for a while that is still even doing the rounds today with various people even remixing it into comedic songs and very recently - even comedic deep fakes have been made of him.

After ten years of first watching the initial interview clip, seeing Kai's story resurface in the media had been somewhat of a little more personal one for me though because what I'd most remembered him for, or so I'm thinking, was not his unforgettable hatchet event description - but another quote that I heard him say during one interview where he'd referred to those with such similar lives as his as being the ones that society generally doesn't notice if they were to go missing, and are the type of people that often no-one comes looking for. At least I've always remembered it in my head as him that had said that anyway - in which before I'd even spoken with Kai it would flash back in my mind ever year or so.

Having watched the Netflix documentary that had come out about him, I'd also come to find that only months after the initial interview in 2013 that he'd also been imprisoned for murder relating to a separate and controversial incident just months afterwards. Kai had been befriended by New Jersey attorney Joseph Galfy in Times Square, New York, who'd offered Kai to hang out and have a place to stay there before Kai continued his journey to New Jersey.

Kai claims to have been drugged and sexual assaulted by the attorney, and despite him claiming to be a victim of rape - there seems to be many questionable factors into the true authenticity of the investigations, with investigators of the case going on to say that any sexual activity between them both had been consensual, although no real forensic investigation had been done on any of the items which could have held up Kai's story.

There are of course a lot of factors to take into account, not only from what I'd noticed myself in the documentary, but also on some of the things that Kai has been able to correct me on whilst in the process of writing this book.

Whilst watching the documentary, I guess like many I'd genuinely thought that I'd been learning about Kai's journey, but really it's not since our exchanges of messages that he's helped shed a light on why many are calling it out as a biased production with questionable statements and false recollections of events. But whether positive or negative, truth or lies, at the very least its format does a good job perhaps unintentionally of revealing two very different perspectives of people and the world.

Kai's initial media interview before he was arrested and charged with murder had brought out a lot of good in people once they'd seen it, and after calling out on the news report that he was looking for a surfboard to use - many had reached out to help him, not just in getting a board but in other ways too, and it was great to see that it had appeared that a lot of love was shown by the many people that had gravitated towards him.

However, it had been more than obvious in some of the clips recorded of him that for some it was just a gimmick, a party and a chance to meet a recent star. Saying that though, despite some of those moments being obvious in the documentary Kai claims that most of the people that reached out to him had done so through the purest of intentions. Still though, as those reading this book will have likely gathered - I know all the too well the side-effects of being someone that others might look at in a somewhat predatory or exploitative way if they think that nobody is looking out for you.

The documentary hasn't just revealed the many bright lights and kind spirits of this world, as well as a one-love 'if I eat then you eat' mentality that Kai would embrace with some of the homeless people around, many being in a much more vulnerable position than himself - but it has also shone a spotlight on how abuse claims can be so disregarded not only by active and influential people within the justice system - but also by passing commentators and talking heads such as those in the documentary that are quick to label such a person like Kai as a fraud or a psychopath without having any real understanding of his trauma or his life.

With that comes the overlooking of vulnerabilities and the experiences that it can bring - as well as how a person does their best to navigate through life with such undealt traumas that they've never had the time to work through, talk about and truly process whilst going through many of their experiences.

During the first half of the documentary - some of the people from the production agency that had started to work with Kai were detailing their surprises and shock at some of the 'edgy' behaviours that they'd claimed to have seen him displaying upon getting him to stay in a hotel. It became clear that they were picking up somehow on Kai's symptoms of Post Traumatic Stress Disorder, yet the clear tones of shock and surprise show how it simply isn't always recognised for what it is, with those experiencing it often simply labelled by those people as crazy whilst many barriers can go up to them too.

But having written this, perhaps it's overlooked whether or not the fact that people were actively out there searching for Kai had any further implications to his own mental health. Could you imagine the moments that can happen whilst being completely oblivious to the fact that so many people were trying to track you down, in what essentially could become a real-life episode of the Truman Show?

Perhaps it's easy to forget that to much of a degree Kai was still relatively a young man when this particular series of events had happened in his life, and perhaps being whisked away in cars and put in hotel rooms by reporters and producers from TV companies had been a bizarre experience in itself to get his head around anyway. One would imagine so.

It's all too easy to over-emphasise and fail to look past a person's trauma, or even the heightened energy levels that it can bring - which at times has its positives. But once again there's too often a lack of acknowledgement and respect for the events that have caused them in the first place, which some people condescendingly go on to label such people as crazy, dangerous, loose cannons and a variety of other ignorant put-downs which often make people be perceived by some as a threat, or simply not worthy of being treated on a level playing field to others around them.

Even having the hatchet in his bag had brought him much flack by some commentators, and before hearing the real reason myself why Kai had a hatchet in his rucksack - even I'd presumed wrongly myself too.

Completely unspoken of in the documentary, and whilst media commentators were making jokes based on the fact that Kai was a hitchhiker with a hatchet, Kai explains in our communications that he'd been using it to chop wood for a camping trip up in a remote location that he was going to in Northern California.

Perhaps the fact that he was on his way camping to a remote location hadn't been spoken about in the public near enough, where even I'd presumed wrong that it seemed practical for self-defence in dangerous situations and had to be corrected to avoid completely misrepresenting Kai and his real intentions within this chapter.

Not that I ever was the type of person to glamourise weapons, but what about those homeless people that don't feel safe out there in the open on their own anyway? In some of my own days homeless and out on my own as an adult it was a rock inside two socks that had been my form of portable anxiety relief in that sense, and at certain times it had not only meant the difference between feeling a better chance of survival in whatever situation would arise - but also the difference in getting just a few minutes quality sleep or not when I simply didn't know what was coming from around the corner.

As a teenage runaway in the nineties and eventually finding what was a slightly safer part of the west end for me to stay despite the obvious risks, vulnerabilities, and experiences - I'd been relatively lucky compared to many others growing up in such circumstances, more so in today's world.

There were always risks whilst out there, but I think things have become that bit more lawless over the last two decades. As for the sleep deprivation though, again that's one huge factor that can be often overlooked when people think about homelessness and the daily effects of it. Perhaps something for some people to contemplate on the next time they see somebody appearing a bit not with it or 'out there' and might automatically put it down to drugs. Unless you know anything about drugs it's possible to get it wrong I believe. Anyway, back to the topic at hand.

Despite the fact that many of Kai's supporters likely know the practical predicament that he was in at the time, the bitter elements within society are all too obvious once you hear the calls from some that such people with backgrounds from care or homelessness shouldn't seek the same value and respect, shouldn't have the right to defend themselves and that violence, abuse and exploitation isn't something that such people should have the voice to stand up against. Before I carry on, let me remind them they are wrong!

It's not always said so directly and clear-cut though - yet all the evidence is there, such as the current struggle in the UK to get children's homes in safe locations because of the constant outbursts and petitions set up by local residents fearing the worst. Yet when those children have been shoved from pillar to post and dumped into areas rife with exploitation when they have battled tough roads for so long - it's all too easy to point the finger.

There are of course some absolutely great people from both seemingly regular and even some from privileged backgrounds that have nailed it in keeping an open mind in connecting with those from such areas of life in order to learn more and build more authentic social support and safeguarding systems. However, the ignorant and judging scold from what can seem almost opposite mentalities is not just a verbal or immediate event which one can easily knock back afterwards, but it can manifest itself in all sorts of different forms of systemic abuse.

But to me, it's interesting that despite perhaps not the majority by any means, but there are still a significant number of people out there that can watch the entire documentary and still hold such people in a judgingly fearful regard, even after hearing about his life at home as a child which would bring tears to the eyes of anyone with a heart.

What would they have done though? They might not even realise themselves the instinct to protect others that may be inside them. Still though, the ability to trick the viewer can be easily achieved when a documentary contains so much bias that without hearing it for yourself from the source then it's hard to know what to believe.

Before speaking with Kai myself I'd already written here a whole piece regarding what had been said about him during the documentary about his times performing music in a bar. Rightly so, Kai had reminded me not to take everything that was said at face value no matter how polished or respectable anybody might have seemed. I won't go into the specifics of that and will let you hear about his life events from himself through his social media and the book *'Smash, Smash, Smash'* authored by Philip Fairbanks.

But reflecting on what may for some had seemed visible signs of trauma, if even true claims in the documentary at all, it had me thinking of the times when I was attending the conferences and sharing my childhood story whilst promoting *Poems From a Runaway.*

Whilst going through a series of events in my home life that some people will fortunately simply never experience, not only was I trying to promote my book whilst struggling financially - but the things going on in the background were most certainly affecting my mental health at the time, which may have displayed clearly to some.

Even if anyone does understand you at all, if things are extremely dangerous and twisted few want to hear it, and by that point the amount of people that have no clue at all what you're battling with whilst judging you for your circumstances or appearance can make it all even more of a confusing place to be.

Before that though, breakdowns in my twenties had largely come about from pure exhaustion and long-term attempts to get myself out of homelessness. For much part it really did feel like I was completely trapped outside of the system where the longer I'd been struggling with no identification or any traceable history the more often I'd encounter technicalities or rules that would make it near impossible at times to get work, a normal place to live or create any sort of life that I was seeing people around me seem to have.

At certain points I'd simply find the struggle simply too exhausting despite being able to just about get by from the odd short-term job or from busking during the worst of it, but putting my all into my music performances every time never really helped with that either once I'd started feeling the tiredness creep into my bones.

It's really not for me to analyse where Kai's headspace was at that point, and perhaps rather than take what you hear about in the documentary regarding some events at face value, perhaps take a look at his social media to see what his response to the whole thing is, but their claims of breakdowns had got me thinking about some of my own experiences at least.

I've had a few of my own every now and then, and it's a lonely and completely embarrassing place to be for sure once you know that you can't undo certain emotional outbursts that others have witnessed - but sometimes life can just take its toll eventually for some. It's all good and well using cliches such as 'keep on trying' and 'your nearly there' which in essence are positive and useful quotes - but until you've felt the concoction of physical exhaustion, sleep deprivation and emotional turmoil for yourself then perhaps it simply appears much easier than it actually is for some out there currently battling with mental health or homelessness.

Without those certain spirits about that can understand what you're going though and will reach out and step into your reality to help calm down the hopeless thoughts, psychotic-effects and feelings of suicide which happen during such breakdowns - it can be simply left to grow inside of a person. We really do need more of those people around that are willing to connect with those going through such experiences if we're going to be a society that truly stands against the amounts of needless suicide.

As for the death of Joseph Galfry, the murder charges against Kai and the events leading up to it all - perhaps it brings up many overlooked elements of what can easily be painted by some as a black-and-white clear-cut situation. Of course, from a legal standpoint it's important to note that I'm only speculating as a typical internet observer and someone that has swapped a few messages with Kai - however, perhaps some of opinions and feelings of those having walked similar paths such as being in care or experiencing homelessness are more valid than often given credit for.

Kai had explained to police investigators after getting charged how they'd both hung out together having eaten and drank beers before Kai had felt tired and had passed out on a bed.

Upon waking up in the morning Kai hadn't put two-and-two together at first when he'd seen signs that something had happened, but just hadn't realised at that point.

He then left Galfry's place that day after being brought a train ticket at the station and was seen on CCTV giving him a thank you hug goodbye which had brought much controversy in the documentary as to exactly why he'd returned back to Galfry's place that evening when his initial meeting with a friend that he'd planned just didn't go on to happen.

Having needing a place to sleep again that evening - Kai states that he'd had taken up Galfry's offer to return if he needed to, in which at some point he'd found himself waking on the floor with Galfry attempting to perform a sex act on him. Although the exact details are a bit murky - the situation eventually resulted in Galfry's death which had been considered by the post-mortem as a somewhat brutal one. As for what people can consider brutal or dangerous though, perhaps much of Kai's story sheds a light on how all too easy it is to overlook the immediate state of mind of someone when needing to defend themselves in such a situation – in the grand scheme of things it only plays into the hands of those with the typical abuser mindset – the ethos that if you dare react or protest to any mistreatment then you'll be branded violent, aggressive and dangerous. Essentially, it's the abuse of anti-violence quotes and pure deflection.

I couldn't help but notice too in the documentary that some of the investigators seemed to be ever so smug and proud of the fact that they found the meeting on the train station CCTV, as if they'd found a trump card to completely dismiss his claim of sexual abuse. But in reality it does nothing to give a true reflection of how a person can react to either known and unknown traumas, and it does nothing to educate others about how these sorts of events are played out often between the lines through psychological manipulation and centuries-long established trickery.

It had been revealed however by Jessob Reisbeck, the reporter that had initially discovered Kai during the hitchhiking incident and seems to have been one of his main advocates in the documentary - that at some point after going off the radar for a while Kai had posted on his Facebook page about the abuse events, and in quite specific detail too.

Those that haven't gone through such abuse, or haven't focused their awareness of it might not be able to fully understand how much of the workings of it are played out between the lines yet are open in plain sight which for some can be all too easy to dismiss off as seemingly normal and regular moments.

Even when a person either mildly suspects or fully knows something not quite right is going on - even the baffling reactions of people around can stun and shock a person enough to leave them in an unknowingly bewildered and spellbound state. It's all too easy afterwards to reflect on would have, should have and could have - in which to outside commentators unaware of the actual processes that have occurred during such events it's easy to be fobbed off and mocked by those having never been through either abuse or the whistleblowing of it themselves.

Although I've written in *Poems From a Runaway* about one of my events regarding being molested at thirteen years old and certainly intoxicated but also possibly spiked, perhaps now is the time to try and brave it and to be honest with the world about my own life experiences and admit that it wasn't the only time in those years that it had happened to me. There were other times too, in which I remember one particular event where I'd been led to a hotel under the pretence of being brough pizza, and although I'd certainly started putting up barriers after knowing what I'd actually been led there for, it had caused me to get the heck out of there.

However, it may have appeared on CCTV afterwards that I was leaving the hotel with a look of no concern, but inside I'd been mentally stunned and knew that I had to get far away.

Again, one of the biggest battles in spotting and uprooting abuse is knowing that predators take these sorts of psychological effects into consideration, often more than others do to it seems, and obviously for the completely wrong reasons which is one of the oldest tricks in the book for covering up abuse.

Upon hearing Kai's description of what had happened I couldn't help but feel goosebumps in relation to a place that I'd lived at before whilst myself being on the road.

Sometimes people can seem friendly and charitable, but something can unmask within some people when they know that nobody is looking out for you, and if you're in desperate need. Yes, men can be exploited too! And there's nothing emasculating you need feel when the game has been engineered against you.

People finding themselves homeless can end up in all sorts of exploitative situations and it's all too easy to ask why a person goes back to such places but when they have nowhere else and no-one else at the time to turn to, no money and they're just finding it hard to battle the constant knock-on effects of it all.

Sometimes you're just simply too tired of fighting absolutely everything and will take any opportunity of respite that you can. A lot of people imagine themselves being invincible if certain situations had happened to them, "Oh well if that was me then I'd blah, blah, blah."

No offence – I get it, but until you've actually been there then in many ways it's just expression of misunderstanding and ego, fantasy and a denial of real human vulnerabilities and the predatory intelligence to exploit them.

It's another reason those from such backgrounds as leaving care or finding themselves homeless are extremely vulnerable to groups and cults that claim that they are going out of their way to support people only to become entrapped, exploited and abused in one form or another.

But going back to Kai's story, for those that choose to see it the evidence is clear in the documentary regarding law enforcement officers and prosecutors that there seems to be more of a leaning of getting a sense of pride for simply solving the crime and progressing their own career goals rather than trying to understand it from a more humane perspective. In all fairness to them, perhaps in some ways they see it as an efficient mental shortcut to go about their jobs, but too many people suffer at the hands of that and perhaps if they'd have connected with him how they'd have liked to have been treated themselves then perhaps they'd have got more thorough depth and answers eventually to the whole story.

I couldn't help but feel towards the end of the police interview featured in the documentary that Kai was being clearly scapegoated and in subtle ways mentally tortured by the two police officers in the room at that time.

Having observed it the dynamics had just seemed a little weird. There was Kai trying to tell his story the best that he could in an obviously traumatic situation to two police officers that in my eyes were showing signs of emotional disconnection, even seeming to smirk at the fact that he was asking for some water - in which a cup was already there and so he didn't get the couple of minutes break that they might have thought that he'd wanted.

Obviously concerned and distraught, upon the interview ending Kai had asked two simple questions regarding his potential sentencing. The first question was understandably hard to answer for the officers upon asking how long they think he'd get in jail, of which they stated they were unable to answer. But his second question was simply asking if the death penalty was in place in the state that they were in, a reasonable thing to ask, in which they then walked out of the room purposefully leaving him in limbo and stating that they couldn't talk to him anymore, which despite some could claim is merely part of a legal process in the video it just seemed a somewhat cold and neglectful way of treating a person in such a situation.

Despite there needing to be some sort of professional ground as well as boundaries, treating such cases like a game should never be seen as normal. Perhaps for those wanting to make genuine improvements to professional systems then however harsh and judgmental it can sound perhaps we need to start leaving that sort of behaviour and disconnection in the playground if we want to truly rid our culture of established toxicity.

Again, it's one of the very essences of this book which perhaps in its own way weaves the unintended message that if society ignores its treatment towards such people on the fringes then it is only left to grow and breed into the rest of culture. The signs and stories are sadly all too often there to see, we're worth acknowledging!

Witnessing such events makes me wonder – is narcissism currently winning some sort of war on human consciousness? But when you keep seeing it affecting the world that you find yourself in it can become a constant drama for those that wish to live in peace without it. Many of us go on to try and find our own paths which brings its own unique and memorable moments, but as the world labels you a drifter or a free spirit the reasons why some of us are living that life is often far from how it can appear - which people can presume that it's simply because you haven't chosen or tried the other ways.

When I was out there busking a lot more than I do now, people used to come up to me and tell me that they'd wished they had the life that I had. Sure, it was nice that they'd respected me enough to say that - but it was as if they'd thought that I simply didn't want to work and pay bills and had made a point of dropping out, which was never truly the case.

I think I was always trying to build something from the ground up in order to maintain some control of my life at least. Like it is for many people - it was always more of a struggle than I thought that it would be - but I knew that apart from a lack of income then only I was largely the one responsible for what went wrong. I couldn't really get stitched up when I was busking, which wasn't always the case even in places where private security teams came along.

Maybe something to think about though when you wonder why some people go on the paths that they do. Still, it's fair to say that on other levels people are just roaming the earth outside of the cage and living their existence to experience the real riches that money can't buy. It's all got its pros and cons I suppose, but like much in life it's not all bad.

As for Kai's imprisonment regarding the Joseph Galfry case, I'm certainly not trying to take away from the fact that Galfry's death had been a tragic and misfortunate event, especially for those that loved him. But beyond that, and whatever you're opinion on that particular case - perhaps we really do need to start acknowledging that such people like Kai and myself are vulnerable to those in society that think that they've got the right to do whatever they want to some of us, often even expecting to continue on with their lives with no consequences whatsoever and often having more advocates for their voices than the victims of exploitation or sexual abuse.

Without choosing to recognise those existing social dynamics which in many ways are similar to racism - the exploitation and abuse towards such people in society will only create further damage before anything is ever done to prevent those things from happening in the first place.

It's a money machine for the justice system in many ways whilst often those perpetuating the abuse go on living their lives as if nothing had ever happened, and even protected with people or influential community members having their backs. Abuse survivors however go on to battle a whole host of mental health effects and trust issues which might sound simple when put into words but can have phenomenal impacts on their life experiences.

As for Kai, despite a jury given no real option from the judge but to conclude with a guilty verdict that had completely disregarded his claims of being able to prove that he was drugged and sexual abused by Galfry, he was sentenced to fifty-seven years in prison of which he's to serve at least eighty-five percent of it.

It seems that there are many highly questionable things to consider regarding the whole set up of the proceedings, even regarding his own defence counsel. I hadn't even realised myself how deep it had got until Kai had pointed out to me that recently a federal judge held that there was a "sufficiently alleged conspiracy" between the alleged-rapist's brother, the prosecutor, and Kai's defence counsel to rig his trial.

For the real nitty gritty of his story you'll have to read more in the book *'Smash, Smash, Smash'* - but Kai makes it publicly aware that he's still currently in the process of appealing his case, something which you can find updates on regularly from a Facebook page called *'Kai The Hitchhikers blog'*.

Please make sure if you're supporting any fundraisers for Kai's appeal that you do your research to make sure it's only from links officially supported by him - as even his story has been open to yet more exploitation through online scammers and opportunists.

As well as appealing the legal decisions of his own case, Kai has also dedicated his time inside jail in attempting to create substantial change regarding the laws on allowing sex offenders into government roles. Many abuse campaigners will know what I mean when I say that it could be seen by some as a social media sacrifice to be challenging such organised forces, but Kai finds himself in a somewhat unique position to be able to make use of his fame where perhaps this really could be something that could make waves, and he's got this far at least.

I'm well aware that everyone deserves a second chance, but perhaps we have to be brutally honest about the effects of bystanding and corruption when it comes to thinking about the ethical leanings of key decision makers.

Hopefully the ball keeps rolling, certainly a beautiful gift to leave to the world and if for any reason it doesn't happen then he's certainly inspired many of an upcoming generation to make a stand against a system that protects the abusers, and abuses the abused. Well done lad!

Chapter Thirteen – a memoir to lighten the mood.

After what has certainly been a somewhat deep an intense chapter and a look into how the system can react to the issues of homelessness and sexual abuse, perhaps it's time to throw something into the mix to lighten up the mood a little.

Going over some of the issues in the last chapter has meant that I've certainly needed a few hours break to rejuvenate whilst writing this - so there's a part of me that's conscious of its heaviness also from a reader's perspective too.

See, despite this book being about some of the unseen sides of mental health and homelessness, of course there's also been the good times as well, not only in London but also down in Brighton where I'd go on to live in a squatted mansion with a toilet literally fit for a king. Hang in there, I'll explain.

It was probably a good thing that I'd branched off from a friend that I was going to the anti-war demonstrations with every week outside the factory up the road, for their sake really because everything had seemed a little intense generally with both the police attention at the demonstrations in Brighton, and with what was happening at the time with the court case against the police officers in London.

Having being in the activist café a lot at some point and explaining my situation to a guy that I'd got to know a little over time - he'd explained to me that his friends had just opened a squat up the road and thought that they'd be up for letting me live there if I got to meet them, and so we made our way a mile or so up to the other end of town where along the way he'd explained that it was an old mansion. Upon getting there I'd come to discover what was still quite a big looking place, but with the building stretching out a lot to the back from the front - it had first appeared much deceivingly smaller.

Upon being welcomed in and introduced to the four people that were there that all went on to become good friends - it hadn't taken long to discover that this place really was a mansion, still sporting it's beautiful stained-glass light fittings, dumbwaiters, safes, a huge marble staircase with alcoves inside where statues once stood, and next to it a secret door in the marble wall halfway up the staircase, in which you could only just about notice that it was there.

Although we ourselves used a small kitchen that was at the back of the house - the main kitchen itself would have put many restaurants to shame with the size that it was. Among the many massive rooms was a ballroom as well as one with a grand piano and lavish wallpaper with painted murals of cherubs playing horns on the ceiling. But the most truly unique feature of all?

King Edwards personal toilet!

Although originally built in 1828 (the mansion, not the toilet) from 1896 the Duke of Fife had lived there with his wife - Princess Louise who was the daughter of King Edward VII. Downstairs near where the safe was had been his own personal toilet for when he'd visited. Despite obviously being a very old toilet with its wooden seat and wooden fittings encasing the cistern and its huge pully-chain, how could I not make sure I've ticked another unique box ay? Enough said, but it brings a new meaning to a saying – a royal flush.

Big rooms and plenty of space had been one of the upsides of squatting at times when I was growing up in London, although this time apart from when we were sleeping - the majority of our time in there was spent together hanging out in a small room above the front porch which is called a 'sunroom' apparently. It was a nice little space with beautiful white sequined seat coverings which went all around the room, but also gave a beautiful view of the sea just across the road.

Knowing that people would worry about it getting vandalized by squatters however, we even made a point of approaching the neighbours to tell them that we weren't going to see any damage caused to the property and that they were always welcome to come in and have a look around the place if they'd fancied it.

There was only a small crew of us there throughout it all really, which was a wise decision made by the two lads that had initially opened the place, and it had become obvious that they were wise to do so once the media had all turned up.

We certainly weren't expecting it, but one of our group had come in with a local newspaper headline poster, and in big black letters it read '£1.5M FREELOADERS TAKE OVER BRIGHTON MANSION' or something or other.

It wasn't long before reporters had turned up to the door to ask us questions about why we were living there, and if we were squatting there to make any sort of political statement. Not that we were there to send any sort of message, but someone had printed out a sign explaining that we knew the historical importance of the house and wouldn't cause any damage to it.

Upon answering to reporters through the letterbox - our already well-spoken middle-class friend had now exaggerated the poshness in his voice which had likely made us appear much more 'middle-clarse'.

Having noticed a whole row of journalists with cameras outside of the house during those two particular days - I think we all presumed that we'd ducked down below the windows in time not be photographed, despite having one or two "did they get us then?" moments.

It had turned out thought that we were in a few of the mainstream newspapers the next day, in which there in the Daily Mail was a photo of myself looking out of the window, and also of another of our group.

Ironically, despite photographing the two most working-class lads among us, our friend had certainly contributed towards giving them a different impression where in the papers they'd written how one of the neighbors had said "They look like scruffy students with combat trousers and baggy jumpers with holes in."

"But they're very polite and well-spoken. They seem like your typical middle-class dropouts. Their parents are probably doctors or architects."

I find that part hilarious really, as my parents have certainly never been in the world's where doctors and architects mingle.

I knew the reference to combat trousers was likely about myself though, or possible another one of us, but it's funny how people can have completely different impressions of someone depending on the environment and situations that they're currently in.

All the media hype soon died down after a few days however, in which we were served an eviction notice which stated that we had to leave on Christmas Eve. But we certainly made good use of the building during the rest of our time there where one night we'd put on a party, but it certainly wasn't a rave.

One of our group living there had been giving people tours of the building along with explaining its history, and in the room where the grand piano was in we'd lit some logs on the fireplace and got a few people to perform on it for the evening. It definitely felt a little posh, but it was something different and some really nice people were there in which I even caved in eventually to people asking me to play a set on the guitar, which I'm glad I did afterwards.

We'd been given the eviction notice quite quickly which wasn't a surprise considering the attention on us at the time, and it gave us six weeks to move out until Christmas eve when the bailiffs would turn up. When eviction day came, we'd decided to move out on the quiet before the morning, and having all gone our own ways at the time, most of us with new girlfriends - I'd go on to spend that Christmas with the now mother of my daughter, who gave birth to our wonderful daughter around nine months later.

Just thought I'd share that little light memoir after what's been much reflection on heavier topics.

Peace.

Chapter Fourteen – Targeting and money machines.

Having already written my thoughts on the story of one person with a history of homelessness, I'd also planned to have featured someone else in this section, whose website and videos I'd reviewed before things taking a sour and unexpected turn. However, due to how me and this person met, I do cover some of the spookier aspects of targeted harassment in this chapter.

Despite some intense conflict happening between me and this person - he did actually have some good points about how the homeless can be expected to rebuild their lives from what can too often be substandard conditions.

It would be a shame to have to completely re-write this chapter, so I'll salvage what I can because I think there's some really good points in here!

It must be around a decade or so by now since I first crossed paths with this person on Youtube within the targeted individual community when I was finding myself on a quest for answers as to some of the times I'd felt I'd been followed, or spooky events happening where I was living.

Despite the effects of those more odd and baffling events, of which some I've mentioned earlier – much of it had brought a lot of paranoia and trauma in itself. Back in those days people like us were still on some sort of quest in learning of why people were behaving the ways we least expected towards us.

Looking back on it all brings up a lot of emotions. Like the times I haven't been feeling so invincible anymore, realising that perhaps I might of rocked more boats than I'd been aware of whilst being a self-styled writer and campaigner. I'd also wondered if I'd even failed to spot when I was being completely manipulated, and that all of this time despite growing up on the streets of London that I should have known better if I was being had over.

Still, hands up, for my times on the street or whatnot perhaps I really was naive about some parts of society, assuming that I simply thought like everyone else did, perhaps forgetting that I grew up on a different program to those that simply don't understand me.

When you're isolated you feel different, and you really shouldn't because deep down we know that we're not - but unfortunately some of us are simply now living with this feeling too deeply integrated in us during our most isolating times.

I'd rather not be putting myself in this 'ostracized' box, but for me – acknowledging what I'd never really considered as a social status was all a bit of a personal wake-up call as to why some of my life events have unfolded in the ways that they have.

As for the person I was covering in this chapter, well, many of us on these forums were claiming that dodgy and baffling things were happening to them, but there hadn't been too many stories I'd found resonating with my own like this person's had.

I'd stayed lowkey on the videos and forums mostly as a silent observer, mainly because I'd got put off from some of the comments about people being harassed by aliens, followed by the illuminati and voice-to-skull technology put inside of people's heads - which wasn't really at all providing me any signposts to any of the actual answers that I was looking for.

With no real public information about narcissism, stalking and psychopathy on the internet at the time – many people were clutching at straws for answers inside of the 'targeted individual' movement.

As I've mentioned earlier on in the book, sometimes those forums we go looking for answers in are full of all kinds of wacky conspiracy theories, but some of the things that this person was saying had sounded too familiar to some of my own experiences. Despite these sorts of forums merely being a sort of pit-stop service station for those in a long-term quest for answers - it would often take many more years and journeys for those like me to start really getting any.

I hadn't even known at the time until years later that he'd grown up in a world seemingly not too different from my own, in which I was to find that he'd too been on the streets from a young age and was largely out on his own in life.

Those from much more bonded families can easily fail to understand how it really is to grow and develop in such circumstances. Not that it doesn't have its valuable advantages - but not everyone can truly appreciate what it's like to navigate and battle life pretty much completely out on your own if they've never been exposed to it.

Despite being careful to trust what my contributor-come-saboteur has been expressing online, I've no doubt that his coverage of how homeless systems can operate could indeed be revealing what is a worldwide problem too often caused by corruption - or a loss of original vision from the amounts of government money that can be claimed by those that know how to play the funding game all too well.

It's a sensitive topic to approach however, because the last thing I want to do is give a bad name to some of the brilliant and spirit-filled people and charities that are doing wonders to help change people's lives. Still though, the exploitation can be played out on so many levels that it can be difficult in some places to know where it begins and where it ends.

For some charities, the problems are merely systematic failings that make it much harder for many people to simply find a stepping-stone out of their situation, and thus at times any sense of blame is not always with the organisation itself but the economic structures that it lays within - like a game of 'funding bingo' so to speak, where many charities are bound in all sorts of rules and red tape in order to obtain any financial support from the government.

Having currently gone back to his Youtube channel to take a deep dive into his content, even this first video that I'd randomly clicked on regarding his experiences of trying to get into shelters whilst homeless were raising many valid points about everything that is wrong with what many of us presume is a social system that provides accessible and set-in-stone emergency accommodation to those that need it.

In the video where he shares his past experiences, he details well of how extremely limited support for homeless people without drug addictions can be, where in some towns there was simply nowhere to go unless he'd falsely claimed to have an addiction himself.

Back when I was a young teen on the streets, one or two people even joked about me getting a urine sample from an addict in order to get emergency accommodation, so I can believe it.

Of course, such services are vital in supporting people in our communities, but what my source speaks about here is one of the biggest problems I've seen within the homeless and emergency housing system in the UK too.

One of my biggest questions ever to this world is - why do we so often tend to focus much more on the devastating after-effects of a situation instead of putting our efforts into prevention?

Generally though, and with it seeming more often than not, with the main emphasis on homelessness being around drug addiction - often the only places available for those without savings and references whilst finding themselves desperately in need are often ram-packed hostels or somewhat neglected supporting housing schemes where quite often in both cases heroin and other hard drugs are so rife that you can smell it engrained into the walls and carpets.

A person may find themselves fortunate if they do find housing support through other means which enables them to function in a reasonably stable environment. Whilst living in one particular hostel for around a year in London when I was sixteen, which wasn't my only time in one, thinking about it now - the numbers of different people and their problems in there had been a somewhat realistic reflection of the amount of support that is out there for those that have both fell out of the system but never did have any drug addictions like crack cocaine and heroin.

In most of the times that I'd managed to get emergency housing support I'd nearly always be in the five to twenty percent of people that weren't hard drug users wherever I was living. Sometimes even some of the older non-addicts simply leave a hostel after a day or two and go on to live on the streets because the sort of lifestyle that the 'one size fits all' approach to homelessness and housing too often breeds hard drug culture and even at times prostitution.

You'd think it would spur someone on enough to want to do all they could to move on as soon as possible, but again - with the extra rental costs for what can often be a way of life that prevents any normality

such as cooking or being able to have a visitor come and see you once
in a while, not only can it become depressing but also a financially
near-impossible task to get out of for some, and as my source explains
– that's if those people can actually get any emergency housing help to
start with.

Despite realising that my source is, or was - prone to holding a
vendetta against people - he also goes on to explain how at times there
are people working within the homeless system that are in it for the
wrong reasons, not always merely just individuals, but at times whole
teams too.

With being unaware of my source's sour relationships, it would be
unfair for me to comment on the individual cases that he's referring
to. But it does happen.

For some it's seen as a cushy job with no manual labour, and for
others it might just be another stepping stone on their career path. But
it seems that all too often the emergency housing system can at times
be a complete charade.

Sure, I've met some amazing and beautiful people during my times of
need whilst growing up, but despite the appearance of everybody
banding together in the name of goodness and charity – sometimes the
same old monkey-politics and needless scapegoating still plays out in
these worlds where often people wouldn't expect it.

When these sorts of places are run with a genuine value for people
they can of course make all of the difference in somebody progressing
on with their lives. But left by a whole society unchallenged - perhaps
some simply can't see that the emergency housing system can in many
ways be just like a prison or an institution, not pro-actively encouraging
people to live regular and normal lives but instead creating a whole
new set of barriers which can often do nothing more than result in a
young person becoming completely institutionalized.

There are likely many more young people growing up in today's world like I did, and I'd found myself extremely fortunate too at times to be inspired to have some sort of work ethic at least. Without that though I would have likely gone on to the flat I eventually moved into in Hackney with no real domestic skills such as cooking and cleaning. In fact – despite helping set-up and take down the markets once in a blue moon as well as working on an Evening standard stall as a runaway in London, sweeping up the warehouse floors before and after the squat parties had pretty much been the first time that I'd picked up a broom.

Similarly to the guy I was writing about in this chapter, having seen various different elements of the homeless support system across the UK, it had become obvious to me over time that instead of focusing on developing peoples skills in a way which reintegrates them back into society – instead, the general approach across the board seems to have grown ever more into property investments which are funded by addition discretionary housing benefit money all under the name of extra support - but people can be left for years in some places with no genuine doorway back into normal life and society.

In today's world of promoting property investments to those with the money to invest, some could argue that the concept of being able to pay off mortgages and gain lucrative properties through government money has completely corrupted the homeless support system, as well as other important public services such as children's homes and care homes for the elderly.

It's without a shadow of a doubt that one of the main reasons that abuse towards the vulnerable seems to have exploded is because the ethos that it's about the money in many ways can seep into the work culture - causing people not to connect truly with those that they're working with but instead just turning up to work day-in day-out to collect their paychecks, in which naturally it creates the sense of division and an institutionalized reality.

Many homeless people have found their lives isolated enough already and could do with nothing more than people just treating them with a common respect, which doesn't always happen.

Again, that's no disregard to some of the brilliant people that I've met along my journey, but I'm sure even those people working on the other side of the desk could elaborate more on what I'm saying here.

In many ways my sources videos have provided me much reassurance that a lot of what I feel and have experienced simply isn't all just in my own head, even if I do feel iffy trusting everything that he's saying. He describes of how some people use those that they are working with as an emotional punchbag to offload their own personal gripe onto, which is something that should never be happening in such professional realms - but all too often is.

It's something that I've been saying a lot recently, and perhaps one of the biggest drivers of creating this book - the claim of what I'm shouting out loud that people like myself that have experienced homelessness and have done it alone from a young age are experiencing what is a sadistic and abusive phenomenon that needs to be acknowledged, and currently at large really isn't.

Whether it's the responses we expect telling us just to get over it, or that people in other countries could have it much worse is often merely just the immediate denial to acknowledge it, and in some senses a lack of vision of creating a meaningful homeless support system that genuinely does what it says on the tin and perhaps raises social questions way beyond that.

Until these sorts of systems are re-designed by those that can truly understand such a life - not much will change for the immediate future on a wider level, which is why it's every more important these days for community support workers, employers looking for young talent and even sports teams to be taking a punt from time to time to meet some of the young people that find themselves living in these sorts of places.

It's those sorts of opportunities that can have such a massive impact on a young person's perspective of life going forward, and especially for their confidence in a world where they too often can be misunderstood or scapegoated.

Some of the things my source says in his videos do in fact do a good job of detailing how much the general ethos towards homelessness has changed rapidly over the last two decades - of which upon reflection the contrast is obvious.

Since economic recessions and government cuts have happened, what had once been to some degree open doors which would serve great numbers of those in need, with today's landscape having almost completely changed these days, things are now generally a lot more closed-off and privatised - where ticking certain boxes for government funding can too often prioritize over what can be an efficient and less rigid way of providing support.

It's reminds me a lot of how some of my struggles in adult life whilst homeless had seemed simply bizarre - where at one point I'd been so desperate for somewhere to stay that even a night shelter would have helped me get some rest at least, even though I'd generally always avoid using them growing up.

I'd simply been exhausted from spending almost a week without any sleep at the time, and so I called up the number for one of the biggest UK housing charities who told me that in order to get into a night shelter that I had to be seen out on the streets sleeping rough by a team of outreach workers that would come to see me once I gave the charity my location.

Things would have probably been a little easier to swallow if I'd been able to go myself to speak with them or simply sit and wait there, but the regulations in place during that time meant that I literally had to be seen inside of a blanket or sleeping bag on the street, 'bedded down' as they call it, something that I hadn't done at the time for over a decade.

I was in my late twenties at this point too having found myself back in London with no savings after a relationship breakdown, and at that point it had just felt a huge step backwards to be out sleeping on the streets after spending years trying to carve a completely different sort of life for myself.

When things had got this bad though I'd usually find a cheap backpacker's hostel or something for a few nights, but having exhausted absolutely everything by that point and seeking advice from a number of support services it had literally been my only option at the time.

For those ignorantly judging me for being in such a situation and likely presume that I hadn't been working, only a short while before this I'd been employed until my hours had got suddenly cut - leaving me with what merely felt like pocket money.

Sure I struggle getting work, but part of that is because so many choose to instantly disregard any skills and experience that you might have anyway if they've heard of a struggling past, and might even ask themselves more questions once they see that there's gaps in your official work history - yet fail to understand why.

I'm certainly not saying that I haven't had some of my own faults get in the way too, but it's all too easy for people to link homelessness with bad news.

And so that night I 'bedded down' as they call it, in plain sight for the world to see - although by this point, I simply hadn't wanted anyone to see my face in case anyone recognised me from the campaigning that I'd been doing.

After waiting all night- nobody had turned up though, in which the next day I called the charity back up again and they assured me that the team would definitely come to see that night, but after doing it all again, still nobody did.

Upon calling one further time on the third day, they'd go on to tell me that because the side of the street that I was on was technically outside of some sort of boundary - that it had meant they were unable to assist me. It's a situation I've actually attempted and failed at several times in attempts to get emergency accommodation.

Has this really become our way of helping those in need of a place to stay in this country? A 'computer says no' mentality that means many people are unknowingly to most getting completely disregarded and exhausted whilst others presume that all the help that they need is out there for them?

I think it's time that homeless people and those estranged from their families get more recognition for the things that they've learned quite early in life. Whilst it's often our types that were getting reported or arrested sometimes needlessly whilst growing up in the care or in homeless systems, many more seemingly regular people can go all of their lives and stay under the radar without learning the consequences of their actions.

If you're looking for genuine advocates of systemic failings and abuse that don't show any signs of frustrations, mental health effects or wear-and-tear then you'll be extremely lucky to find any, and sorry to disappoint you but I don't think that there's too many around.

Unlike Kai the hitchhiker which I featured a couple of chapters ago - not everyone from these backgrounds has that same sort of charisma about them that can draw people in, especially for those showing visible signs of their trauma, mental health problems or their struggles.

But for whatever impulsive and defensive quotes that some from more non-confrontational environments might find shocking or edgy, perhaps more people need to understand what sort of a life can lead people to react with that bite in their bark, but also that those wearing their hearts on their sleeves are more vulnerable to coming out with such reactions which others portraying a more stable image can easily manipulate and use against them.

The more people speak their truths, the more information there is out there regarding the systemic failing of how we approach homelessness these days.

Not everyone agrees with taking issue with some of the only homeless charities out there, but for those thinking that it could be done more authentically - then it's something which really needs to be acknowledged if we are going to live in a genuinely civil and spirit-filled society, instead of one based on steamroller-economics, facades and corruption.

The more people have spoken out about the misuse of charity funding, the more people continue to ask - Where is all the money going?

For those on ground level directly witnessing the neglect of some of these places it becomes obvious that it can be an important question to ask.

Perhaps how the efficiency of our homeless systems have huge impacts on society is underestimated. Maybe it's time we admit that the system in general could do with more people in key positions that have the lived experience. Not to have them as a 'lived experience' token, but for genuine thorough change.

It's true that we need a new format of supporting such people for any of it to really be genuine and efficient. When the true voices of homelessness are counted for then perhaps a symbiosis of both the people with lived experience of homelessness and those with the resources and influence will lead to authentic and meaningful change.

The current issue we face regarding those with lived experience entering such positions is that they find themselves getting cut out of the deal. It's what I've seen all of my life even in the digital realms that make out to be progressive.

Sadly, a lot of us have gotten used to the fact that we'll be automatically thrown under the bus or to the bottom of the pile. Thank goodness for those shouting out that vent that frustration with a passion - in what unknowingly to many can for some be a desperate attempt of having some sort of authentic recognition on this planet without being exploited and abused by the people that make out that they are helping them.

In another video my source explains how in one homeless shelter that he stayed at of how he saw the staff working there and acting cruel and belittling to the homeless service users, at times even provoking those staying there in order to get a response and get them kicked out.

I've seen the same thing happen myself here in the UK. Again, those with no self-control over their own abusive elements know all too well how the homeless person will likely either not be believed or simply will be automatically disregarded.

"Bro, why would someone that's trying to help the homeless and do good just kick you out for no reason" he says - as an example of what can be a typical reaction, and as he explains – all too often those with certain mental health issues or traumas that are easily provoked will be the first ones targeted as an excuse for such abuse.

Mixing the concepts of homelessness and business is something that I've always been well aware in today's financially-structure world.

Perhaps some of these shelters and hostels really do start off with the purest of intentions, but as people hand in bids for what can be at times lucrative contract deals - what had started out once as a genuine spirit of charity and helping homeless people change their lives can quickly become corrupted to the point where financial investors specifically seek out avenues to receive various forms of government money and public funding which homelessness, mental health problems and drug addictions are far too often the scapegoats for such 'business' opportunities.

Again, that's no discredit to the genuinely passionate people and organisations that do fantastic work, but let's be under no illusions that we need to keep our eyes wide open for the exploitation of such concepts.

Later on in the video my source brings up the controversial subject of 'gangstalking' which despite the stigma attached to the topic - which in turn could completely ruin the creditability of this book - I've decided to cover it still as I've already dipped my toe into this world just a few chapters ago.

But perhaps it's a subject that might be worth looking at - in which perhaps even I myself have a few important questions to ask because for a number of years now I've been highly suspicious of some of the outcomes of my life.

Did my protesting days and perhaps some of my youthful and impulsive acts in the past eventually catch up with me? Am I actually on some sort of blacklist?

Understandably for anybody like myself that goes on to feel shadow-banned or stitched up at almost every turn, those sorts of things are all too easy to overthink especially when you actually have been through some weird stuff.

It's important to note though that whilst covering the subject of mobbing, the criminal world and groups that partake in psychological abuse – my source literally takes off his hat and gives a big shoutout to those people and organisations that are genuine about their work helping the homeless and would know all too well about the financial corruption that he's talking about. He also states how the corruption was so rampant that he'd found himself going on a journey in being able to heal and trust again those that were genuinely out to help him, something that I'm all too familiar with myself.

In another video my source talks about his more positive experiences of working with organisations that gave him the opportunity to become an advocate for homeless people - as well as witnessing them make organized efforts to amplify the voice of those with lived experienced of such a past.

He goes on in the same video to detail a situation that I'm all too familiar with myself, and that's people coming in and simply railroading over those like myself to get in on the action and use manipulation tactics to muscle us out of roles, something which employers and other decision makers fall all too easily for - and something that happens to those like myself all too often.

When it happens time after time it's easy to lose confidence, especially if others outside of the situation presume that it's because you haven't been trying to stand up for yourself, which for many couldn't be further from the truth. A very degrading feeling to say the least.

Sure, those going through the thick of it can be labelled as aggressive or crazy afterwards when really, they're just naturally reacting to being stitched up by people yet again - and how dare we have the right to react and have feelings about any of it at all they say. They'd never admit that they think like that though for most part.

My sources talk of programs and giving those that have experienced homelessness more authentic opportunities that help integrate them back into the community really gets me thinking a bit though. It's been great to see that here in the UK there are a few of the business chains taking steps to help integrate people from such lives back into a world that rewards their hard work and efforts and helps them feel respected.

It's something that certainly needs to happen more, and similarly to the recent acknowledgment by some UK councils of the stigma in society faced by care leavers, which make up a quarter of the homeless population, perhaps it's time to widen the scope and stand up for the other three quarters too that might not have the same privilege.

Personally, I'd love to see something similar to the 'Big Issue' taken to the next level. For all of its uses and genuine opportunity of helping homeless people - I'm talking something completely next level where people can not only learn new skills to help them create products and opportunity - but utilize and improve on the unique ones that they may already have.

Homeless people are too often fobbed off as having no skills - yet have people even tried to see what sort of magic happens when you put somebody into their element along with some basic tips to help them get started along the way? A vision for the future no doubt once the 'grab what you can' crews in powerful circles have backed off from us all a little bit.

Watching my sources videos have given me a chance to reflect on what really in essence is a system that by fault creates more drug addicts and criminals than it really needs to.

I've been saying for years that some of these places are like factory farms, and a good tip for anybody with such a place in their local area that can at times breed anti-social behavior because of the pure concoction that happens within our 'one size fits all' emergency accommodation structure – perhaps it's worth googling who owns the place and what sort of characters are involved in running it.

There are of course some brilliant and bright people in the world helping the homeless, but perhaps a sharp eye on corruption is the last barrier in giving such genuine organisations any hope of further existing.

Also, having thought about how our emergency housing structure can be for many people experiencing it these days - it's far too easy for hostels to become places known for corruption, or a place to make money selling drugs. One could argue in some 'supported housing' projects how deep the corruption really gets.

I've certainly had my own questions in some places that I've been quick to get away from only to continue on my journey of trying to find another way out of homelessness.

For such places which can house both newly homeless, those experiencing it on and off as well as the long-term homeless that you'll find on the streets - perhaps the lack of normality is often overlooked, where some people's problems can be so severe that it means a place where nobody cooks, or nobody learns to - and the same for cleaning or having any normal and healthy life goals.

It's easy to forget that for somebody such as a care leaver or another person estranged from their family that these can often be the sorts of worlds such people can find themselves in if they're out on their own.

Sure, there are places which break that mould, but as far as I can see from what I'm hearing over recent years it's certainly not a situation that's improving - with the homeless being yet another sector of society that is exploited even on business levels that are now fully integrated with handshakes, perhaps at times with friends from the council and such. There are no conspiracy theories at times when you're talking about small towns where everyone knows each other, just facts.

I wish I had all of the answers to improve it, and maybe I can help towards providing a few at least, but the whole structure needs a radical shake up from its current exploitative elements which are too often at play. Many bridges need to be built to enable the recognition and inclusion of such people back in society, perhaps it's something we need to fight for, and this book here is in its own way playing its little part in all of that, but here's a big thanks to those that have helped inspire it.

Chapter Fifteen – Roadmaps forward

Without meaning to sound too negative, let's be honest here, society is broken and in need of much repair.

It's clear to many that it's certainly not just those experiencing mental health issues and homelessness that are feeling the effects of what can sometimes feel a world that's struggled to keep in check it's more narcissistic elements.

Most of us know by now that what we thought was going to be a digital age of ultimate connectivity and freedom has turned out more to be a sort of algorithm-controlled hyper-fuelled megamarket where there's a whole lot of stuff there that you want but most of the time you have no real clue why - until you've learned about dopamine and neuromarketing.

The more that we've lived behind our phones and our laptops the more that we've got used to seeing superficially polished images, which it might not be too controversial to ask the question – is it seeping into our culture and psyche to some degree more these days?

Are we simply getting too used to a world where so much isn't quite what it says on the tin? Where exteriors and imposed impressions count for everything? And what really are the effects of it? Are we simply forgetting how much cognitive sorcery is being used in today's ever-expanding technological world?

Despite having all of the resources at hand and being told otherwise, are we being inspired to just simply follow the current narratives instead of thinking for ourselves. It's a comfortable yet hollow place to be, where little energy is used on emotional processing - and so an image template is used as a go-to reference for quicker system filing so to speak. Autopilot.

Sometimes people tell me that it's a waste of time trying to get people to understand, and that the world's never going to change because people don't want to, but perhaps some of us are left with no other option than to at least keep trying to amplify our voices and experiences.

Maybe among the many different sorts of people that I know, even the activist types and new-age hippies can find it in themselves to accept that improving on our deeper understanding of different people, including the homeless and those with mental health issues, really is a part of raising our consciousness to much degree because then as a unit we'd be accepting the flaws of the very great thing that we're all a part of.

For those who band about quotes of peace, love and unity without much depth, then there's no real 'one love' until we're able to empathically connect with those around us from all walks of life. Until then - 'one love' is only applicable in selective cliques.

But there's much to be said about the current framework here in the UK which is there to prevent those like me from falling out of the system. From my own personal experiences - when trying to escape homelessness it's obvious that many people are just crammed into whatever shithole has been ran by whichever person has their hands in whatever pies.

Nearly all of the places with problems with hard drug use I found were either completely dodgy and neglected, or simply too institutionalized with no real focus on helping a person believe they can achieve more than what they've so far been able to. Too often it's simply a money machine, a factory farm.

Although I did see a couple of people in hostels going to college whilst I was growing up, for me personally I'd simply never been encouraged to study or work, which might have turned out to be a difficult task anyway with the extraordinary amount of housing benefit that was being paid.

Don't get me wrong, people really need the support...but it has to be more than simply drug-addiction management templates and being linked with the justice system. Some of us that found ourselves in that world wanted a much better life than that, not that we really knew it when we were young and unguided, but largely in many places I just saw people getting left to it whilst at the same time never being able to have the chance to afford to save and move on from some of these places.

Sure, there's some legit and brilliant organisations doing much needed work, especially with the under twenty-fives, but I do believe there needs to be a different message sent to homeless people and more genuine encouragement and support that they can be just the same as anyone else, instead of the set-in-stone patronizing mentality that without words tells us that people think they're not capable and they're not welcome.

It would be fair to say that some might need a little more time and patience than others, and even to say that some are simply too far gone down the line. Not that we should use that as an excuse to give up on them though, but there really is still a lot of young and talented people out there that could have a much more wholesome experience if the world had simply looked into their souls a little more.

I felt I needed to explain that because of the all-too-easy "Ah he can get a hostel can't he?" quotes that I know some will say, whilst those explaining the many dire circumstances that are all too common in broken Britain's defunct housing and mental health framework will often be met with the "well beggars can't be choosers" mentality which renders any actual barriers completely invisible to the eyes of some.

In today's current framework, many people will come off the street only to then live in a completely new sort of survival mode, and one still far from the reality of normal and functional living.

Everyone has their own unique stories too, but all too often those from realities not too far from my own are rarely seen for our stories I think. But then again, is anyone? We're never seen as the people battling mental health problems, or people who've gone through severe traumas, or someone who's lost their family, or someone that was abused as a kid, or someone who just got shat on by those in their lives, or someone with schizophrenia, or someone who grew old and nobody was really there for them.

I don't think we zoom in enough to look at or think about those things enough sometimes, and we can see someone as homeless and make such basic presumptions based on no real depth of thinking. They're simply homeless, apparently.

But generally, in regards to our housing system, mental health system and policing - it's clear that we need a lot more people in positions that have actually been through such life positions and battles. That's to no discredit at all to the housing workers having to encounter angry people, or psychologically damaging stories mental health workers might hear, or the dangerous situations that police officers can find themselves in.

But I'm not sure how much I can take of seeing urgent calls from the heart and what I first had thought were perfectly rational things to be concerned about simply go over some people's heads.

At the end of the day, those going to mental health services and other places for whatever support they need shouldn't have to be battling and standing there asking everybody why they're just simply not taken seriously.

It's yet another thing overlooked that leads this world to become more fake. Those clued up enough know that the system is screwed and will tell you to make sure you tell them the very worst of your symptoms when visiting mental health services, and exaggerate them if you need to in order to receive support.

It's a real shame that people feel that they have to do that, and believe it or not despite being a right blagger as a kid on the streets with all sorts of lies and stories, it had only been for survival really - and as soon as I grew up a bit I hadn't needn't to do it anymore.

As like many others though, as the world changes and time goes by - perhaps my own journey into mental health support will get better one day.

Going through the stuff that I've mentioned in this book certainly has its affects which impact my day to day living as well as my relationships. Trust is a big one in my world - in which it's hard to know these days who's really wanting to see you do well and who's throwing banana skins in front of you. All you can is keep your faith that you're not alone and embrace the spiritual reminders when you find yourself slipping!

As for employment, well I know in this current climate that not everyone is going to care. I suppose this book isn't for those that see those working for them as merely numbers that can be easily replaced, but those that understand how true and genuine team harmony, healthy work dynamics, along with true leadership in management can help massively boost workplace productivity and moral.

I suppose what they need to realise is, is that if they're unaware of - or ignoring such dynamics, then they're probably missing the rest of the stuff that comes with it such as theft of produce, sabotage and deceiving work practices. Not only that - but noticing such behaviours could in fact lift up a bed of other such toxic practices including racism, sexism, misogyny and inappropriate behaviours among other things.

Seriously, those people with their quirks that many aren't taking seriously, perhaps they're underestimated, perhaps it's worth your time listening to their opinion because like I said before - it's amazing what you can discover when people automatically assume that just because you've been financially poor that you're standards and morals must be too.

But perhaps the wear-and-tear and degrees of mental health affects wouldn't be so great and obvious in some - not only because of the systemic problems that I've mentioned in this book, but also because of the journey of young people that grew up in care and then left it like I did, unsure of their reality or future, and in many ways out on their own.

Some of you may already be aware of the huge shortage in foster parents in the UK, and it's certainly not a new issue. In fact - decisions are made regarding where children will be living likely on a daily basis - in which I look back at the many times that I'd been told by social workers that I'd have to live in a children's home simply because there were no foster parents available.

Despite some of the staff in the homes that I lived in doing their best to make the experience as homely as possible, it never truly could be in many senses. Many of the rules and restrictions are necessary - but there's simply too much red tape for a young person to grow up with any homely sense of reality.

Robust safeguards are certainly needed in children's homes, because the young people living in them do become targets of exploitation. But my message here is that we need more foster parents to provide places for the children that need them.

Such as is the case with homelessness, fostering has also been known to be exploited for the financial gain – which is why it's great to see fostering panels made up of care experienced people that get to thoroughly review those that apply to foster, in attempts to screen out those that may not quite be suitable for the role.

Negatives aside, if you think that you could help provide a comfortable and welcoming home, as well as a person they can open up to for a young person to heal through their trauma, then let me warn you that it won't always be easy but you'll be doing the world a great favour and literally changing lives.

I can tell you from direct experience, even if for some reason the whole relationship turns sour that they'll still remember you and the important moments, of which some even you might underestimate.

Putting aside the necessary short-term and long-term foster parents that look after young people that are in some sort of transitional period in their lives, perhaps it's worth noting that children and young people in care don't just need a place to stay until their sixteen and have officially left the legal system - but like the rest of us they need to feel welcomed, valued and an included member of the environment around them.

I can't give enough respect to the amazing folk out there that tell those young people growing up that they don't just have to disappear off away - but have somewhere that they can come back to and are welcomed in for life.

Sure, many of our struggles have led to character-building and developing other ways of thinking, but there's simply too many young people leaving the care system and developing all sorts of mental health issues which could have so easily been avoided if they hadn't felt so alone in the world.

"Well, we all have problems, don't we?" some people might say, but it goes little way in showing an understanding of what it's like to constantly observe others that seem to have a much more solid and natural sense of family connection.

Many will still go on to live fruitful, successful and loved lives - however, everyone's past and current circumstances are always different and unique, and even in worlds where most people have little support, some still have much more than others.

The one thing I found with social media, Twitter in particular, was that the adult stories of many care leavers were in many ways completely unaccounted for. I completely understand the need for inspiring stories and celebrations of successful and famous care leavers, but I often found my insights and reflections about the fact that so many homeless people I met were care leavers had felt largely ignored by the world of social workers that I'd found myself in.

Perhaps they saw it as very 'fringe' and just part of my weird and wacky life experience. But no, do they even realise that care leavers make up twenty five percent of the homeless population, as well as almost twenty-five percent of the adult prison population?

It seems that the majority of people have so far completely rejected my ethos of inclusion - whenever I've brought up the subject, almost like the story of the roaming care leaver is a non-existent one, yet all too common.

Sure, I'm somewhat a different kettle of fish, I get that. My days in London and Brighton introduced me to many creatives, artists and big thinkers. And so getting myself on social media, making my websites and creating books is just something that I've gone on to do in my journey, but there are many more just like me that have the exact same, if not greater talents and passions that could have created so much magic if only life had just been that little bit more normal, consisting of the relationship dynamics that many people take completely for granted.

It's one reason that I urge anyone that feels that they've got natural empathy to consider fostering a child or a teenager. Every young person will come with their own unique set of circumstances and challenges and it's certainly not an easy road - but in my own journey I believe some of the deepest parts of my character were built on the times that I truly felt included and brought into the normal family activities and celebrations whilst I'd been in foster care.

It something takes great people and a lot of patience though, and it's certainly not something that just anyone can do. But for those who live by knowing that the real treasures of life are unseen by the eyes and felt deep in the spirit - it can be yet another meaningful journey that grows yet more depths of wholesomeness.

Simply knowing as an adult growing up into the world that there's familiar people that you can go back to for a chat over a cup of tea, or to celebrate a birthday or a wedding with, or all of those things that both young and adult care leavers only dream about can make all of the difference between a young person building their lives from a stable and supported base - to a depressing reality of feeling that nobody cares about them, often becoming an ever-growing candidate for much needed psychiatric care and medication.

As for those that go on for years struggling, battling known or unknown mental health problems and learning to adapt to their circumstances, they may appear as choosing to be drifters in what can often be actually a lonely journey of struggle.

Those moments that come by partying with new-found friends are all well and needed for someone like me who'd find themselves in many such situations in my twenties, but perhaps now I realise that I always felt that I was missing that something deeper in my life, that real sense of deep connection I suppose.

It's something that all of us struggle with, but too often are those going through it alone underestimated for the mountains they've climbed at times. Some get through it better than others, but some never get the chance to truly rest at all.

Many have got used to it I suppose, and rightly so, there's no point whining because it is what it is, but at the same time I feel the world needs to know and take a moment to think what it's like to have that sort of depression affecting you for what is for many people all of their lives.

It's not meant to be a pity party or feeling like weakened victims - but instead be recognised as people that have learned to carry so many feelings of neglect, confusion, pain and of being completely misunderstood by the world around us that perhaps we're more hardcore and resilient than a lot of people give us credit for.

But that sort of respect needs to not only translate into community conversations - but also in places such as the workplace, the police station and the mental health department among many other places.

Even though people don't always say it in words but often simply through actions, reactions and ignorance - the echo is all too loud of people saying "what, that homeless person? What do they know?" - when in fact despite perhaps not knowing about how to apply for a mortgage, or not being able to read and write, or not having a prim and clean picket fence garden - perhaps it's time that those having lived such turbulent lives are finally respected for the real stuff that they've seen, and the battles that they've been through.

See, here we have there on show for you all to see the results and symptoms of the many things that are wrong with society - yet instead of listening to people and bringing them into situations and folds we deem them as useless and less capable of someone with a seemingly regular past.

We know deep down that it's not the case, and I'm hoping that despite not having much financial success at all to date that the books I've self-published so far and my attempts of marketing are clear signs of some sort of average potential at least.

If people like myself can do all of this on their own and self-taught, then imagine how far we could go if people actually got behind us, welcomed us into their realities and embraced what we had to offer. It's just a somewhat limbo place to be at times when your life becomes moving around for whatever reason and you've not developed those natural roots and networks of people that feel familiar with you - which is the challenge those like me face when putting on events, creating projects or launching our own businesses.

It's one reason the recent social media connections with groups, projects and meet-up events for care leavers have been vital for the healing of many people over the last few years, as well as organisations such as The Rees Foundation that help care leavers across the UK, as many others face some of the stigmas or situations that I've mentioned in the book - if not more severely for those with other stories.

I suppose deep down I just want more people to understand the battles we face, and the feeling that can arise of feeling that people don't accept us for who we are. It might come across as playing the victim to some people, but those battles are deep when people for whatever reason are feeling estranged from their families.

Essentially, it's about just making sure that our interactions with such people are genuine and spiritually connective. It's the refusal to be a part of the systemic scapegoating, and it's accepting to step up to be people that want to truly uplift the substance in our surroundings. Be that at home, work or wherever else.

A note from the author

I really hope that you've enjoyed reading this book. It's certainly been an interesting journey for me writing it and going through the whole process.

There'd been a few niggling doubts along the way whether this book would be valued, but if anything, the delay of this book was likely for a reason, and to tell me otherwise.

Whether part of my book really was leaked at some point, or if was simply on hold and waiting for the world to be ready for it – I believe that now they are. We're all on the same page here, I think.

Hopefully my writings have inspired some others to think outside of the box when it comes to how support services, homeless hostels and the like can massively affect a person's outcome depending on how they're ran. We need less institutionalisation and more connection. Regarding young people in care, and those going through the criminal justice system or facing homelessness, often we're placing young people from one institutionalised setting to another.

It's hard not to drift off into conspiracy-thinking when realising how set-in-stone our justice systems, mental health systems and emergency housing systems are.

But saying that, meaningful change doesn't happen overnight. Hopefully some day people within those systems able to make change will pick up this book and in whatever way they can actually make some sort of difference to someone's life simply by understanding them a little better and putting themselves in the other person's shoes.

So, a huge thanks to those that have supported me along the way, whether it being at any stage of my personal life, the production and release of *Poems From a Runaway,* or even those supporting the very book that you're reading now – and especially to all of those sharing the message. It's great to know that there's a tribe of people that understand us out there. Never let anyone make you forget that!

You can help support this book by mentioning it to anybody working in professional supporting roles, or simply anyone you see holding any unthought-out prejudices against the homeless, drifters or those with mental health problems. Tell them to grab a copy, remind them that there really are some riches and knowledge to be found from places where some people presume that nothing really grows.

I'd also like to send a shoutout to Kia the hitchhiker for his time and contribution to this book. Please do check out his book *'Smash, Smash, Smash: The True Story Of Kai The Hitchhiker'* by Philip Fairbanks.

You can also visit his official Facebook group at
https://www.facebook.com/groups/officialkaihitchhiker

Once again, a huge shout-out to anyone that values, supports and shares my work for others to discover. It really means a lot. Big Love. Change is possible. Over and out.

One last thing....

You'll never walk alone.

~ 217 ~

BENWESTWOODUK.COM